PUNK ROCK THEOLOGY

Punk Rock Theology

NATHAN PROPER

XULON PRESS

Xulon Press
2301 Lucien Way #415
Maitland, FL 32751
407.339.4217
www.xulonpress.com

Paperback ISBN-13: 978-1-6628-6407-0
Ebook ISBN-13: 978-1-6628-6408-7

Table of Contents

Just Read It

I want to change the way we read the Bible. For most of us, that means reading it at all. I live in a world with no shortage of Bible teachers and preachers, each with their own interpretation. You can watch in person and on video, listen to radio and podcasts, or read books and blogs. That sounds like a great thing, but I think we are too comfortable letting the so-called experts do the reading and accepting whatever they say.

This book is my attempt to convince you to pick it up and read it yourself. I want to show you an approach I call Punk Rock Theology. It just means thinking for yourself and letting God speak for Himself. Don't automatically conform to what some influential leader says. Don't mindlessly repeat what someone taught you as a child. God gave you a brain and he wants you to use it. He gave us the Bible for a reason, and He will use it to teach you about your own life if you just give Him a chance.

I know I'm weird. Not everyone gets excited over ancient grammar or the social conventions of historical cultures. I understand that part. But why do we act like you have to be a hardcore theology nerd to read the Bible? God did not inspire and preserve His Word for thousands of years just for the handful of intellectuals who geek out over Greek and Hebrew. The Bible is accessible to anyone and applicable to everyone. Popular opinion seems to disagree. I blame my fellow Bible nerds for that. When we teach from the perspective of things we learned through years of study, we imply you need all that background to find these insights. Just because God speaks to theology nerds through nerdy theology doesn't make that the only option. He knows you personally and can speak to you as you are.

John Eldredge said, "Story is the language of the heart." From books to movies to television to newspapers to social media, we all love stories. Modern neuroscience finds storytelling the most effective form of communication. God knew that all along, so when He wanted to reveal how the world really works, He gave us more than a bunch of rules. From cover to cover, the Bible is full of stories. Even the unexciting lists of names and laws are details of the story, while poetic sections like Psalms and Proverbs offer a glimpse into the characters' thoughts and emotions. God, the expert storyteller, weaves all these bizarre stories into the grand story of His plan to save us from ourselves. Not only are they case studies in human behavior, but they reveal His work behind the scenes in millions of lives across thousands of years. When Jesus finally came to show us what God is really like, He told even more stories.

One of the greatest lessons I ever learned in reading the Bible (oddly enough, at a concert) is finding yourself in the story. I don't mean finding a specific character you can relate to so much as recognizing the humanity in the narrative. Remember that these characters are real people living real lives in the real world. Put yourself in their shoes. Imagine what it feels like to hear the news or witness the spectacles that rock their worlds. Consider how you would have faced the same dilemmas and terrifying circumstances. We often overlook the gravity of those details, especially when we know how the story ends.

Some question the Bible's authenticity, but I can barely take that argument seriously anymore. No book in history has as much physical evidence to back up its claims. Archaeology has already verified thousands of names, dates, and places that people formerly questioned, and the list keeps growing. Historical texts confirm that a shocking percentage of the actual words have never changed to fit a new understanding. The overwhelming majority of what we consider "history" rests on comparatively flimsy evidence.

A more legitimate objection is the Bible's dirty little secret: if you study Scripture well enough, you can find ways to make it say anything you want. Over the years, men have used God's Word to justify countless atrocities. You cannot necessarily trust what you hear from a preacher, an interesting article, a YouTube video, a social media post, or a book (including this one). I don't expect you to take my word for anything. You should read the Bible for yourself and see what it says. Acts 17 has a story that praises a group of people for doing exactly that. This is why I included references for each story so you can check it yourself. If you don't have a Bible, download the *YouVersion* Bible app (or go to Bible. com) and you can read in just about any translation you like. It even has tons of reading plans available to help guide you.

Many people consider the Bible too old and irrelevant for mature intellects of the modern world. This one confuses me. Scripture addresses everything from financial and relational struggles to organizational leadership and civil unrest. Have we somehow evolved beyond that? The stories tell us not only what happened but what always happens. They illustrate the foundational principles that drive human behavior and the world around us. If you take the time to look into it, staggering amounts of modern medical and legal practice were founded directly on Biblical principles. Many essential elements of society, like hospitals, orphanages, and universities, originated from people who took the Bible seriously.

I admit that reading the Bible cover to cover can be intimidating. The whole thing is about 750,000 words, give or take, depending on your translation. For perspective, that is more than the complete *Lord of the Rings* saga but less than the entire *Harry Potter* series. Like those and other book series, you can always read one piece at a time. The big difference is that nothing says you must read the Bible in order (scholars don't even agree on the "right" order). Better yet, you do not have to read the whole thing for God to speak to you. Countless lives have been transformed by one story or even a single verse.

The hard part is internalizing the message and putting it into practice. One of my mentors calls this concept "giving it handles" – moving beyond hearing the story to see how it all applies to your life. That's what I have tried to do here. I have no interest in becoming one more "expert" telling you what it all means. I want to show you an easy way to read the Bible and let it speak to you. I already admitted that I get excited over obscure background details, so don't be surprised when I share some of those because I find them fascinating. Still, I did my best to focus on the plain stories to let the text speak for itself.

If you are already comfortable reading the Bible without my help, feel free to give this book away and read that instead. But if the Bible bores or confuses you, maybe this book can help. Whether these stories are familiar to you or not, take your time reading and see what they have to offer. God put it here for a reason. Let's see what we can find!

Starting Point

Genesis 1

"*In the beginning, God created the heavens and the earth.*" That and "*Let there be light*" are probably the most memorable parts of the Creation story. What you believe about the universe's origin (particularly the people in it) affects your life more than you might realize. That makes this narrative the foundation for the entire Bible.

In short, God made everything. Later Scriptures point out that this means literally *every single thing* that has ever existed or ever will exist. Things we can see and things we cannot. Things we can measure with scientific instruments and things that we can never quantify. God made rocks and air and light and time and magnetism. He also made love and humor and music and intelligence. Sure, Genesis does not list all of those details. Still, the first verse already told us that God created the

Heavens and the Earth, a metaphor for both the intangible and the physical world.

The part where He creates humans deserves special attention since I assume everyone reading this is human. First of all, God has a conversation with Himself about us. Genesis 1:26 says, "*Then God said, 'Let us make man in our image, after our likeness.'*" That single verse, appearing in the very first chapter of the ancient Hebrew Bible, has profound implications. I will not attempt a full explanation of the Trinity. Just acknowledge that we unquestionably have a singular God speaking of Himself in plural pronouns. I highly doubt God has multiple personalities, like Sméagol and Gollum inhabiting the same body and occasionally having conversations. So that plurality is at least worth noting.

Next comes the first poetic segment of the Bible, Genesis 1:27. "*So God created man in His own image, in the image of God He created him, male and female He created them.*" Since God views Himself as plural, creating humanity in His image requires more than one. This single statement affects the rest of the Bible, "*God created man... male and female.*" The Bible was written down by men and addressed primarily to men because it was composed in a patriarchal society. Do not mistake that to mean that women are in any way second-class or not included. Quite often, when the Bible speaks of "man," it encompasses both male and female, as we see here. From the beginning, God bestowed his image upon a male and a female together. No man reflects the whole picture, and no woman does either. We can only display a right portrayal of God by coming together in perfect unity. Sadly, that has probably never happened since Eden and never will this side of Heaven.

Search the Scriptures for descriptions of God and His attributes and character, and you will find many references to maternal behavior. I have no desire to set up some new doctrine or heresy here, but God is more than just our Father. He is also a mother. Where did you think the very concept of motherhood originated? Satan didn't create it. People didn't invent it. God made it, along with the maternal instincts that typically go with it. Look around you. Are compassion, tenderness, intimacy, and nurturing affiliated mostly with men or women? Well, all of those things come from God, and He repeatedly claims those attributes Himself in both the Old and New Testaments. I'm not saying God is a woman. Still, if you want to be precise, I don't think you can claim He is a man, either. The Bible consistently describes Him with masculine pronouns, but that is all the distinction you will find. I doubt we have a word for it, but God is somehow male and female, and yet He is neither male nor female.

I know this is just the first chapter, and we dove straight into confusing theology instead of just a familiar story. I suspect some people will reject me for what I already said and read no further. That's a shame because there is so much to learn here. (In the Bible, that is, not anything I write. If you want to reject me, that's fine; read the Bible instead.)

This story is not a science or history textbook explaining the universe's origin. It is God introducing Himself and His character. One of my earliest mentors said that everything hinges on the first verse. If you accept that "*God created the heavens and the earth*," you should have no problem with anything else the Bible says. A God who can create the physical universe by speaking a word can easily pull off the most mind-boggling miracles.

More importantly, this is a sample of what to expect from God. For one thing, He might not give us all the details. He just summarized the entire universe in one chapter! And don't get hung up on confusing ideas like one God using plural pronouns and how "the image of God" requires both male and female to be complete. God is so far beyond us that human language will never fully and accurately describe Him. These are just some early examples of that challenge. You will find a lot more throughout Scripture.

For now, let's just agree that we will never wholly define God. He is under no obligation to explain Himself to us fully, and I doubt we could remotely understand it if He did. Don't let that discourage you, as though seeking to know Him is a lost cause. On the contrary, it should highlight the significance of what He chooses to tell us. Deuteronomy 29:29 says, *"The secret things belong to the Lord our God, but the things that are revealed belong to us and to our children forever."* We do not and cannot know it all, so what God points out are presumably the essential pieces that He wants us to remember. Don't get hung up on the spots where you wish He would have said more. Focus on taking to heart and living out what He already said. Most of us don't need more knowledge; we need to obey the parts we already know.

Naked in a Garden

Genesis 2:15-25; 3:1-20

Adam and Eve were naked in a garden. A snake convinced Eve to eat an apple that God had told them not to eat, so they got kicked out. That's pretty much the whole story of Eden, as we remember it. Oh, and by the way, every human being for all time is by default a wicked sinner because Adam and Eve ate that fruit. We reduced something as significant as God's original design and the fall of man to a talking snake and an apple. That's a shame because this story has so much more to it. Let's jump right in.

First, let me address the two distinct narratives in Genesis 1 and 2. Chapter 1 gives an overview of the whole creation, and then chapter 2 sort of zooms in closer on the creation of humankind and gives a fuller story of that piece. Some people insist this is a contradiction, which is just silly. Imagine I told you the history of

World War II, saying the Axis fought the Allies and the United States got involved after Pearl Harbor. If I come back later and tell you about Dunkirk and Normandy, would you call that contradicting the first story? Genesis 1 says God created man and woman. Genesis 2 says God created man, put him in a garden, gave him a job to do, gave him a command to follow, and made a woman because He didn't want the man to be alone. It's just a more detailed account of the same story. Some of those details carry a lot of significance, but we blow right by them.

For starters, Adam has a job to do in Eden. Work is not a bad thing. The concept of work and responsibility is created in perfection before sin enters the world. Genesis 2:15 says God assigned him as the caretaker of the garden. This job is surely much easier before complications like weeds and droughts, but it is still a job. Adam also has to name all the animals, which is no small task.

When God brings Eve into the picture, the perfect world includes marriage. As we saw in the last chapter, God designed marriage to mirror His image in the world. Most people seem to miss this: God does not just create a man and a woman, but a husband and a wife. Genesis 2:24 says that this original couple is the basis of all marriage. Jesus himself quotes it in a debate about marriage in Matthew 19. Why does the text describe leaving father and mother when the only people in existence at this point have no father or mother? This line is certainly not about them or for their benefit. Just like that memorable detail of them being naked is not just so we could illustrate them cleverly hidden by bushes and long hair but shows absolute openness and transparency. Part of the reason this story is in the Bible is to teach us what God intends for marriage. The original design has no secrets, no shame, no hidden fears, and nothing whatsoever to hide from each other.

Moving on to the notorious forbidden fruit, did you ever notice that nothing says what kind of fruit it is? I can't speak for the entire world, but I know that growing up in America, it was pretty universally displayed as an apple. I still have no idea why we decided to use that. Genesis says it was pleasant to look at and seemed tasty, which doesn't narrow things down much. Some Bible scholars think it was grapes, which I find more convincing. Grapes, raisins, and wine appear surprisingly often throughout the Bible, and the metaphor of a grapevine is almost overused. Numbers 6 seals the deal for me with the Nazirite vow for people who deliberately wanted to set themselves apart for God's glory.

Verse 4 says, "*As long as they remain under their Nazirite vow, they must not eat anything that comes from the grapevine, not even the seeds or skins.*" (NIV) I suspect that curious stipulation traces back to this forbidden fruit.

Of course, no one can prove it one way or the other, so the specific type of fruit is interesting to consider but not worth arguing over. The critical thing to recognize here is how many people have this definite image of an apple when Scripture does not say what it is. Be very careful interpreting a precise meaning where the Bible does not give us one. One of my early mentors, Chuck Smith, used to say, "Where the Bible is silent, we too must remain silent." That is excellent advice!

In a pattern we have all experienced, a decision that seemed like no big deal—maybe even an outstanding idea—immediately fills them with guilt and shame. Adam and Eve suddenly feel uncomfortable with their nakedness, so they famously make clothes out of fig leaves. On a purely practical level, this could be a horrible idea because sap from fig leaves can burn your skin. (My fellow nerds can Google *furocoumarins* to learn more!) More importantly, the innocence and intimacy they once shared are lost forever. Some commentators suggest that the fig leaves were not merely clothing but a camouflage to hide among the trees. So not only do they want to hide their bodies from each other, but they hope to hide from God, even though that is both impossible and pointless. This moment is the origin of shame and fear, two things that never existed in God's perfect garden.

We easily overlook that God primarily blames Adam, even though the text explicitly says Eve was the one who listened to the snake and chose to eat first. Adam actually tries to throw Eve under the bus and blame the whole thing on her, but God doesn't let him off the hook. Throughout the Bible, Adam always takes the lion's share of the blame when referring to this event. Why is that? I can't fully explain this, but it comes down to responsibility. As far as we know, God never personally told Eve not to eat the fruit. That command was given to Adam in Genesis 2:17 before she existed. Genesis 3:6 says Eve *"gave some* [of the fruit] *to her husband who was with her."* So, Adam was just standing around doing nothing while this snake was tricking his wife into violating their only rule? God said in Genesis 1:28 to take dominion over all animals, so he certainly should have taken charge of this situation. More than that, spiritual authority is a central concept in Scripture. Adam was unquestionably the leader here, which makes him responsible for anything that happened on his watch.

With perfection marred by distrust and rebellion, things God created as gifts immediately become a curse. God tells Adam that work is now a tedious, endless chore. He tells Eve that marriage is now a conflict and power struggle. They both learn that their bodies will now wear out and die. Finally, God kills at least one innocent animal and uses its skin to make garments for Adam and Eve, making this the first instance of death in the world. Things look pretty bleak.

Or do they? Take a closer look at God's response to their sin. First, He comes looking for them in the garden. Rather than waiting for them to return to Him, He seeks them out just as Jesus later comes to Earth to pursue us. Then Genesis 3:15 says there will be hostility between the serpent's offspring and the woman's. The original language uses the term "seed" for offspring, which is significant because nowhere else is a woman described as having a seed. That is always the seed of the man. Most scholars see this as the first hint of a virgin birth. That same verse also predicts the woman's offspring stepping on the serpent's head, another implication of Christ defeating Satan. Finally, God making clothes for Adam and Eve is one of the few places where nearly all Bible commentaries agree. This unidentified animal is considered the first example of substitutionary atonement, where someone else who has done no wrong dies to cover the sins of the guilty. That concept would later be formalized in the law of Moses and eventually fulfilled in the death of Jesus. Sin no sooner enters the world than God reveals His long-range plan to deal with it once and for all.

That plan existed before they even sinned, highlighting one of the most vital elements of this story. We tend to focus on their sin and its results, but I contend this story is more about the original design and what life was like before sin happened. The perfect world included work without toil, marriage without conflict, and intimacy without fear or shame. It all centered on pure fellowship with God and fell apart when people broke that. Humanity has longed for that perfection ever since. Unfortunately, we typically put our energy into chasing the results instead of the source. I believe this is why Jesus said in Matthew 6:33, *"seek first the kingdom of God and his righteousness, and all these things will be added to you."* That is not promising a perfect life, at least not on this side of eternity. Instead, it reorients our perspective to restore the relationship with God first. He is far better at making the other pieces fall into place than you or I will ever be, so why run yourself ragged trying to do it on your own?

Floating Zoo

Genesis 6-9

Some crazy old guy builds a giant boat and manages to get two of every animal on earth onto it. Then a massive flood comes along, but the people and animals on the ship survive, with a rainbow in the sky symbolizing that God loves them. This must be the only version of Noah's Ark that most of us remember. Why else would we use it as a theme to decorate children's nurseries? If you pay close attention to the story, there's a whole lot more to it, and much of it isn't very kid-friendly!

This story is a popular target of skeptics, who pick it apart and call it nothing more than a fairy tale because it is obviously impossible. I won't spend the time to work through all of these arguments, but let's take a moment for the most common one: "You could never fit every species of animal on a boat." For starters, exactly how many animals are we fitting? He doesn't need every *variation*, just every *kind*. Save a pair of canines, and they'll eventually repopulate the world with everything from wolves to chihuahuas. Keep in mind that this isn't a zoo where animals all need individual enclosures to suit their tastes; it's more like cramming everyone into a bomb shelter. If God can convince them to come aboard, He can get them to coexist while they're inside. And while we're at it, who says they're all full-size animals? If I were planning this rescue mission, I would get babies. From elephants to crocodiles to turkeys, baby animals need less space and food.

Regardless of what animals we gather, we still need a lot of space. The thing is, we don't generally realize how big this boat is. God tells Noah to make it 300 cubits long, 50 wide, and 30 tall. Scholars debate how big that cubit is in modern units because there have been a few different standards over the years. The most common conversion is 18 inches so let's use that one. This makes the ark roughly half the size of a Nimitz aircraft carrier, large enough to carry 522 modern railroad cars. Or, if you want to go the geek route, it's about the same size as Battlestar Galactica and only slightly smaller than Godzilla. So, it's a really, really big boat.

But that's the other thing we get wrong about it. It might not be a boat at all but a box. I don't know why we always draw it like a boat with a keel, rudder, bow, and everything. The Bible says nothing about that. It's just an ark. Where else have you heard that term in the Bible (or perhaps in an *Indiana Jones* movie)? The Ark of the Covenant! It's the same word, yet we never imagine that one as a boat. Noah builds a giant box in the desert. He doesn't have to launch it as a boat or navigate it in any way. All it has to do is float when the water shows up. According to modern shipbuilders, a wooden boat of that size would break up in rough seas. I suspect that a giant box (maybe even with some interior walls to add structural support) would be sturdier and easier to build. Come to think of it, the text never mentions any rough seas, just a lot of water. Nothing highlights any wind or waves, so maybe this is smooth sailing. For the sake of Noah's family and all the animals, I sure hope so!

I cannot prove how everything works onboard the ark any more than you can, so my answers are not necessarily correct. But they are *plausible*, and that's the point. You can easily research it yourself, no matter which side of the argument you support. In my experience, it follows a predictable pattern: an objection has several possible explanations, but we can't conclusively prove what happened.

No matter how you work out the logistics, Noah looks like a fool building a giant box to keep animals in while the rest of the world drowns in a global flood. Locals probably consider him a lunatic, and the enormous structure may become a tourist attraction. You would think animals showing up and climbing onboard might convince people to take him seriously, but evidently not. Finally, God sends Noah and all the animals onto the ark seven full days before the flood begins. This final week is the last chance for people to heed the warning and escape the coming judgment. As far as we can tell, no one cares.

At least until it starts raining, and "*all the fountains of the great deep burst forth*," whatever that means! All I know for sure is that there is a lot of water, way more than you could ever get from regular rainstorms. Our nursery scenes never acknowledge the overwhelming death and destruction. God said humanity was so corrupt that he decided to push the reset button and start over. I imagine people trying to climb on Noah's boat/box, screaming and pleading for him to save them. What must that feel like to Noah's family? The Bible describes Noah as righteous, not heartless, so he no doubt feels compassion for the panic and desperation surrounding him. Scripture tells us that God personally shuts the door to close them in. I suspect that is to keep them from jeopardizing everything by trying to let anyone else on.

Every man, woman, and child not on board the ark dies, along with every animal that can't survive 24/7 in deep water. (Why do the sea creatures get a free pass in this global judgment?) Sure, lots of animals could swim for a while, and I assume some people at least cling to floating debris. Even Jack and Rose used a wooden door; in this case, entire trees would be available. But it takes 150 days until the ark even comes to rest and nearly a year until everything is dry enough to come back out. Their biggest problem would not be staying afloat but having supplies to outlast that ordeal.

Even after the flood, when they finally come back out of the ark with a rainbow in the sky, it's not the beautiful picture from our storybooks. There is no giant drain where all of the horrors washed away, leaving behind a pristine, new world. We know the devastation caused by a tsunami or hurricane, and this scene is exponentially worse. If you've ever seen the aftermath of a flood, anywhere that hasn't been actively cleaned by human hands still holds the evidence. You can find debris scattered through the woods years after everything grows back. Does Noah's family have to work around half-rotted carcasses—human and otherwise? Don't forget, the animal scavengers that usually eat things like that died in the same flood. And what is it like to start a new life with no one on the planet but your own family (who just spent over a year cooped up together on a boat)?

We carelessly gloss over these strange and challenging elements when telling this story, but what if these uncomfortable details are essential? As appalling as this magnitude of death and destruction is to us, that is how God feels about sin, and there is no cute and pretty solution. Even when God rescues us from the consequences and spares us from experiencing His wrath, we often still have to deal with the mess it leaves behind. This is reality, whether or not we like it or even understand it.

The New Testament mentions Noah five different times. Each one draws the distinction where Noah listened and obeyed God while everyone else ignored him. It sounds like that is the primary lesson from the whole story. Noah and his building project were a warning to everyone for many years. Swarms of animals showed up and willingly boarded the ark, adding serious credibility to that warning. At the very end, God gave everyone another week to heed the warning and escape the coming judgment. Nonetheless, there *was* a firm time limit. Once God shut the door, no one could get on. It was too late to change their minds.

We are all in the same situation to this very day. God is very patient with us and gives us plenty of warnings and opportunities to respond, but there is a point when it is too late. Jesus said that the future judgment of the world will be just like Noah's flood. Everything will seem fine, and the few people preparing for God's impending judgment will look crazy until it happens. At that moment, it will be too late to change your mind. On a smaller scale, no one can ever guarantee that you will live to see tomorrow. Will you listen to the warning while there is still time and ensure that you and the people you love are safe in God's protection and not left outside to face the wrath?

If You Say So

Genesis 12-22

A shocking percentage of the world's religion traces back to one man. Judaism, Islam, and Christianity all view Abraham as the father of their faith. God promised to turn this desert wanderer into a great nation. He believed it with no evidence simply because God said it and then patiently waited for it to happen. We only know of God speaking to him a handful of times over at least 30 years, probably longer. Still, he obeyed and trusted God through extreme circumstances, even without the benefit of any law or Scripture to reference.

Christians often make the mistake of viewing Abraham as a Christian. He lived a few thousand years too early for that distinction. He was even a few hundred years before God gave the law to Moses and formed the nation of Israel, so we cannot technically call him a Jew either. The man who will eventually be renamed Abraham enters the story as a rather generic pagan. Abram is a Chaldean, a culture of many gods, but when the Lord, the ¨capital G¨ God, speaks to him, it clearly makes an impact. From that day forward, we see no evidence of Abram caring a bit about any of the other gods of his fathers. Instead, he trusts completely in the God who spoke to him personally. I find that particularly impressive because God tells him to leave his country and go somewhere else without naming the destination. I'm not even sure he gets a direction like "go west" or anything. It's more like, "get out of here."

Abram suffers the cruel irony that his name means "exalted father" when he is an old man with no children. His wife particularly feels the sting of that one since everyone assumes it is her fault. Infertility can still consume a woman's identity today, and this is even worse. Sarai lives in a culture where a wife's first duty is to give her husband children, particularly a son, an heir. The primary value of a wife in their society is to look good and make babies. Sarai (whose name means "princess," by the way) has no babies, but she knocks it out of the park in the looks department (more on that later). Despite the thousands of years between them and us, they behave precisely like we still operate today. They label drop-dead gorgeous Sarai based on the only area where she doesn't measure up. As soon as she enters the story, we read, "*Sarai was barren; she had no child.*" (Genesis 11:30)

God has already promised to turn Abram into a great nation. When they arrive in Canaan, He emphasizes the promise and says his descendants will own the land. Having already trusted God enough to leave everything behind and move to literally God-knows-where, Abram accepts the assurance about the future. At least until a famine hits and he heads to Egypt to wait it out, but not without telling Sarai to pretend to be his sister. She is so gorgeous that he fears the Egyptians will kill him to take his wife. So far as we can tell, God never told him to do any of this; it is all Abram's idea. I wonder how he reconciles that against God's promise that he will be a blessing to the entire world and that his descendants (who don't exist yet) will possess the land. If God is right, Abram cannot possibly die from a famine or someone killing him to steal his wife. Once again, he behaves like we still operate today and comes up with a way to handle it himself. Even in light of God's promises that he genuinely believes, fear and worry drive him to create a contingency plan.

Sure enough, they barely arrive before everyone starts raving over how beautiful Sarai is. She winds up taken into Pharaoh's harem while Abram gets all kinds of lavish gifts. God starts punishing Pharaoh for it, and he somehow discovers the truth and yells at Abram for tricking him. In the end, Abram leaves with his life and his wife, along with a substantial boost in wealth from those gifts he got for essentially selling his wife. This story is strange. Was that a good thing? Is that how God was blessing him? How long did that last with Sarai in the harem? How did she feel about all of this? The Bible is awkwardly silent on any of that. It is just a thing that happened.

Abram's life takes off at this point. He and his nephew accumulate servants and livestock until the land cannot support them both. Abram freely gives up the most desirable land and moves away. God already promised that land to his descendants anyway. Later, that same nephew gets taken captive in a war among the local kings. Without hesitation, Abram slaps together a makeshift army and goes to get him back. We have one random nomad going up against the combined armies of four kingdoms, and the battle gets all of one sentence like it's no big deal. Afterward, Abram doesn't even want any of the loot. He trusts God to bless him and won't let these kings get the credit. Curiously, that didn't seem to bother him with the gifts from Pharaoh, but maybe that ordeal taught him a lesson. God promised to bless him so much that he would become a blessing to everyone else in the world. Abram finally knows to trust that promise and stop worrying about anything else that comes up.

But there's still the pesky issue of an heir. This fact troubles Abram to the point that he brings it up right away when God next speaks to him. *"What will you give me, for I continue childless... Behold, you have given me no offspring."* (Genesis 15:2-3) This time God specifically promises him as many offspring as the stars in the sky, and Abram believes Him. Here is the defining moment in Abram's life. The most repeated line of Abram's story comes from this conversation, where Genesis 15:6 says, *"Abram believed the Lord, and He credited it to him as righteousness."* (CSB) God declared Abram righteous for his faith because he believed that God would do what He said.

Modern Christians tend to focus on the story of Isaac and the near-sacrifice (don't worry, we'll cover that in another chapter), and we are rightfully impressed by the faith behind it all. Ironically enough, when the New Testament celebrates the faith of Abraham, it typically points to a moment before he even got that name and long before he ever became a father. Romans, Galatians,

Hebrews, and James all commend Abram for accepting God's promise to give him more descendants than he could count. Pretty remarkable for a guy who was already old enough for Romans 4 to call him as good as dead.

Ultimately, Abraham left his mark on history based on one thing: He believed God. Sure, things went off the rails here and there when he got scared or impatient, and he messed things up as often as he got them right. Still, it collectively taught him the most important lesson any of us can ever learn: God keeps his promises. It might make no sense to us and take way longer than we want it to, but He *always* comes through. That much is true, whether we believe it or not. The real question is whether we genuinely trust God to do what He said just because He said it, without evidence to prove it. Better yet, will we trust Him when all the evidence seems to point in the opposite direction? That is the kind of faith that makes us right with God.

No Laughing Matter

Genesis 16-22

God promises to bless the entire world through His servant Abram and give him as many offspring as the stars in the sky. That is a fantastic promise, and Abram gets tremendous credit for accepting and trusting it. Ten years later, with Abram in his 80s and his wife Sarai not much younger, there is still no sign of any children. Abram is painfully aware that his legacy won't last very long, no matter how greatly God blesses him. Despite genuinely believing God's promises, they decide that He isn't getting the job done and devise an alternative strategy. Their plan works perfectly, right up until it backfires spectacularly!

Sarai volunteers to let Abram sleep with her servant, Hagar, in hopes of having a child through a surrogate. Abram agrees to take one for the team and have sex with a younger woman. Perhaps we shouldn't be too surprised when the effects of that decision threaten to destroy Abram's household. Right on cue, Hagar gets pregnant. The problem is she gets a bit overconfident as the mother to the heir apparent and no longer feels compelled to submit to the old lady. Sarai worsens the issue by openly blaming Abram for what the text clearly states was her idea. Upset with Hagar succeeding where she failed, Sarai makes the pregnant servant so miserable that she runs away. God appears to Hagar in the desert with a promise conspicuously similar to Abram's: He will give her countless offspring through the child she now carries. So, she returns and gives birth to Ishmael.

Abram loves life at this point. God's promise to give him countless descendants who would inherit the land where he lived as a nomad sounded a little crazy for an old man with no kids. With Ishmael in the picture, Abram assumes this must be what God intended all along, and everything is finally on track. We don't know what these years are like for Sarai. Is she as content as Abram, or does she still resent Hagar? Does she accept Ishmael as a son? The Bible simply does not tell us. Instead, the story skips ahead thirteen years to God appearing again to Abram. This time He sets up the covenant of circumcision (which I don't think Abram gets nearly enough credit for instantly accepting). He also changes their names to Abraham and Sarah, as we typically know them.

Most importantly, God explicitly promises Sarah herself will have a son named Isaac to fulfill the promise made so long ago. Abraham falls on his face laughing at this idea because he is now 100 years old, and Sarah is 90. Most people don't even remember this story and only pay attention to God's next visit when Sarah laughs at the same promise. Many even look down on her because she denies laughing when God questions her, which is silly since God obviously knows what she did. Within a year, she bears a son named Isaac, which commentaries usually say means "laughter" as a reference to Sarah laughing. I'm not so sure.

Abraham not only laughed at the idea too, but he did it first. Some commentators spiritualize this in an apparent effort to make "Father Abraham" look better. They claim He laughed out of joy while Sarah laughed in disbelief, but the text makes no such distinction. I honestly see more unbelief from Abraham than from Sarah. The Bible literally says he fell on his face and laughed, even telling God not to bother with another son and just bless Ishmael. When the New Testament looks back on this story, Sarah gets as much credit as Abraham for having faith in God's promise to give them a son.

Isaac's name is technically a verb meaning "someone laughs," which could easily refer to Abraham. God first announced that name before Sarah heard Him, while Abraham was busy laughing. Sarah laughs again when she holds her miracle baby and owns her laughter this time. *"God has made laughter for me; everyone who hears will laugh over me."* (Genesis 21:6). Everyone laughed at this story because people that age having a baby sounds crazy. Abraham and Sarah merely got a head start because God told them before it happened. The Bible never explains Isaac's name, so blaming it on anyone is pointless speculation.

Not surprisingly, Ishmael does not appreciate his new little brother. He spent thirteen years as Abraham's only child, the chief object of his affection. Through no fault of his own, this newcomer suddenly displaces him. His status as the firstborn should have made him the heir, but everyone knows that will be Isaac. Can we please admit how harsh this is for Ishmael? When Sarah sees him mocking her precious baby boy, she throws a fit and tells Abraham to get rid of Hagar and Ishmael. Amazingly, he complies and sends them away, even though he loves Ishmael dearly as his first-born son. Despite Abraham giving them reasonable provisions, they wander aimlessly in the desert and nearly die of exposure before God comes to the rescue to kick off their own legacy. Ishmael goes on to be the father of a nation himself. Still, there is some pretty understandable bad blood between him and Isaac. As in, their descendants are still feuding to this day.

Sometime later (no one knows precisely how long, more on that later), God appears to Abraham again. This time God tells him without warning to sacrifice his only son, Isaac. With Ishmael disinherited, Isaac is technically the only son Abraham has left. More importantly, he is the one God explicitly named to fulfill the promise of countless descendants and a blessing to the entire world. First thing in the morning, they are up and off on a three-day journey to the place where God says to do it. Abraham keeps his mission to himself. Isaac does not know the actual plan, and I doubt Sarah knows why they left.

When they arrive at the spot, they leave the servants behind. Abraham brings fire (presumably a torch or something) and a knife, while Isaac carries the wood the rest of the way. Isaac is smart enough to question what they plan to sacrifice since they have no lamb. Abraham says God will supply the sacrifice. Isaac undoubtedly figures it out by the time Abraham has him tied up and laid on the altar. At the last moment, when Abraham is about to kill Isaac, God speaks up and stops him, essentially saying it was all a test to see if he would obey. Abraham suddenly spots a ram stuck in the bushes by his horns, so he releases Isaac, and they sacrifice the ram together. God reiterates his promise to Abraham about blessing his descendants, and they go home.

How insane is that? What kind of God would do that to someone? What possible reason could there be for it? I definitely do not have all the answers here, but I can help with one piece of it. The biggest problem is that we usually picture this scene with Isaac as a child. Depending on your translation, Abraham calls him "lad" or "boy," but that term simply means an unmarried man under 40. Don't overlook Isaac carrying the wood for the sacrifice. I have no idea how much wood you need to make a big enough fire to burn a human body (and I refuse to research that one), but I contend that a child cannot carry enough. Also, the next event that happens after this story is Sarah dying at 127. She was no older than 91 when Isaac was born, which means Isaac will be at least 36 years old by that point. This whole sacrifice ordeal happens somewhere in the 30 years between weaning Isaac and Sarah dying. Stop picturing a helpless little boy tied up by an old man. Isaac is at least a teenager, more likely in his twenties or thirties. With Abraham a full hundred years older than his son, Isaac could have easily fought him off or outrun him if he wanted to get away.

The ancient understanding of this text has always viewed Isaac as a grown man capable of making his own decision. He willingly consents to the sacrifice because he trusts God's promise, just like his father. Hebrews 11 tells us Abraham trusted that God could—and would frankly have to—resurrect Isaac. Abraham had a track record of making "logical" decisions to protect himself and his legacy, which eventually caused more trouble for him. By this point, he understands that God's word *will* come to pass, no matter how dire the circumstances look along the way. You can be sure that Isaac has heard those stories his entire life, which taught him to trust what God says. God explicitly promised countless descendants would come through Isaac. Isaac has no children yet, so they both know that his story cannot possibly end here on this mountain. One way or another, they will both come home.

Even though this is an actual event that happened to real people, it is also one of the most remarkable prophecies in the entire Bible.

- Isaac was given by his father as a sacrifice, just like Jesus was given by His Father as a sacrifice.
- Isaac carried the wood for the altar, while Jesus carried his cross.
- As far as Abraham was concerned, Isaac was as good as dead for three days until God gave him back. Jesus was physically dead for three days until God brought Him back.

My favorite one is the mountain where it all happened. Remember how Abraham said God would supply the sacrifice? He repeated it after they ultimately sacrificed the ram. Genesis 22:14 says it became a famous saying, *"On the mount of the Lord it shall be provided."* Isn't it odd to say that in the future tense—it *shall be* provided—if this refers to something that already happened in the past? Let's fast-forward through history. A couple thousand years later, Solomon builds the temple to house the presence of God on Earth on this same mountain. Another thousand years later, soldiers crucify Jesus on this same mountain. Many scholars believe it probably happened in virtually the same spot!

Abraham and Isaac are both called prophets, even though we never see either one work miracles or speak God's words to the people. Their lives testify of the faithfulness of God, and their own faith in that God who keeps His promises has echoed for thousands of years for us to remember them still today. You and I have the same potential to leave behind a track record of either trusting God or going our own way. How do you want to be remembered?

Wardrobe Changes

Genesis 37, 39-41

A spoiled kid with a fancy coat endures slavery and imprisonment before eventually leading the most powerful nation in the world. According to Hollywood and Broadway, that pretty well sums up the life of Joseph. We really shouldn't be surprised that the Bible's version of the story goes much deeper. So much, in fact, that this is only part one of Joseph's adventures. If you want to see all of the family drama resolved, prepare to be disappointed.

Joseph does indeed hit the stage as an exceptionally spoiled rich kid. Even in their large, massively wealthy family, 17-year-old Joseph is clearly Dad's favorite. Despite experiencing bitter sibling rivalry in his own past, Jacob (aka Israel) blatantly shows how much he favors Joseph. Enter the famed "coat of many colors." No one knows quite what this is, just that it's unique. It might indeed be colorful in a time and place where that luxury is only for royalty and the ultra-rich. It may be a robe with sleeves, showing the world that he is exempt from manual labor. Regardless of how you envision it, this is an undeniable signal to everyone who sees him that Joseph is more important than all 10 of his older brothers. As if that's not bad enough, he has these not-remotely-subtle dreams where all his brothers and parents bow down to him. Joseph boldly shows up in his fancy coat while the brothers are working and tells them all about it. You can guess how much they appreciate that. At this point, his father rebukes him, and his brothers hate him.

Later, those brothers are tending flocks in the wilderness when Jacob sends Joseph to check on them. Joseph has been hanging out at home (for however long) while they've been working, exposed to the elements. Rather than downplaying that distinction, Joseph wears his special robe to visit them. When they see him coming, they immediately decide to kill him. Seriously, it takes all of one sentence to go from "Here comes Joseph" to "Let's kill him!" Luckily for Joseph, someone realizes that if they sell him instead of killing him, they'll get rid of him *and* get paid, which they like even better. They rip Joseph's coat, dip it in blood, and just show it to Jacob.

They never technically *say* Joseph died; they just let him think it. For twenty years.

Joseph, who probably never did any manual labor in his life, gets sold in the Egyptian slave markets to Potiphar, the captain of Pharaoh's guard. I imagine it takes a while to get the hang of it, but Joseph does exceptional work for his master. So much so that he eventually gets put in charge of everything, leaving Potiphar carefree. By slave standards, Joseph lives the good life. His only problem is that he happens to work for the original desperate housewife, who sets her sights on him.

Potiphar is a high-ranking official, and women are mostly status symbols in this culture, so his wife is probably one of the best-looking women in town. Joseph is roughly twenty years old with a beautiful woman coming onto him and no other prospects in sight, but he flatly rejects her. Nothing ever says he isn't interested, and with his status in the household, he could probably get away with it. Regardless, he refuses to sin against God or betray his master.

Mrs. Potiphar doesn't take no for an answer. She finds (or more likely, orchestrates) a time when she and Joseph are the only ones in the house. She grabs him by his clothes and tries to force herself on him, but Joseph wrestles free and runs out—leaving his garment in her hand. She doesn't handle rejection well and immediately concocts a story to punish him and vindicate herself. She claims Joseph tried to rape her but ran away when she screamed, showing his garment as proof. Slaves dress simply, so it's probably a tunic or something, but the critical thing to realize is he's not wearing layers; it's just this one piece. So, when she has his clothes, it's not like Joseph left a jacket behind. She holds clear evidence that he was naked when he left.

Her story makes Potiphar furious. I can't prove it, but I suspect he's actually angry at his wife. I think he trusts Joseph at least as much as he trusts her, so he's reasonably confident that Joseph is innocent. What bothers him is his wife already made a very public accusation—a prominent person accusing a slave, no less—so his hands are tied. He has no choice but to punish Joseph, who ran his whole household so well that his own life was one big vacation. If Potiphar believed the story, he would simply kill Joseph. A slave could be killed for any reason at all without anyone questioning it. Joseph instead goes to jail, specifically, *the place where the king's prisoners were confined.* (Genesis 39:20) That sounds conspicuously like the place where Potiphar, the captain of Pharaoh's guard, has the most influence to protect him.

Maybe it takes him a while to adapt, or maybe Potiphar put in a good word for him. Whatever the case, Joseph fairs as well in prison as he did in slavery. He serves just as faithfully there and soon becomes a supervisor over the rest of the prisoners. Eventually, Pharaoh's chief cupbearer and chief baker end up in the same prison under Joseph's charge. One night they both have confusing, oddly similar dreams. Such dreams must be significant in their culture because they are upset that no one can interpret them. Joseph assures them that God interprets dreams, so they share the details, and Joseph explains them. In three days, Pharaoh will restore the cupbearer to his position and execute the baker. When everything happens precisely like Joseph said it would, the cupbearer promises to put in a good word to get Joseph out of prison but promptly forgets all about him.

Two years later, Pharaoh has a crazy dream. More accurately, he has two crazy dreams that are also eerily similar. When the local magicians can't interpret the dreams, it finally triggers the cupbearer's memory to mention Joseph. They fetch Joseph from prison, and he promptly tells Pharaoh the same thing he told his former inmates: God will interpret the dream. Which He does, explaining that seven years of plentiful harvests will pale in comparison to seven years of a devastating famine that will follow. Everyone in the room is undoubtedly stunned when this slave goes a step beyond dream interpretation. Having learned a thing or two about management in the last 13 years, Joseph suggests a way to prepare and survive the famine. He was in the dungeon a couple of hours ago, and now he dares to instruct Pharaoh, the man they worship as a living god. Far from rebuking Joseph's boldness, Pharaoh recognizes the wisdom in the suggestion. He orders Joseph to carry out his plan, promoting him to the palace with power and status second only to himself across all of Egypt.

Joseph's life has seen as many changes as his wardrobe, despite never initiating or choosing those changes himself. He once had a coat that showed how special and privileged he was, but his brothers tore it away and used it to deceive his father. He became a slave with a simple garment, and his master's wife tore it away and used it to deceive Potiphar. Both cases were more than just a piece of clothing but a symbol of stripping his identity away. He was then a prisoner in rags, but this time he changed those for clean clothes to stand before Pharaoh, who soon dressed him in fine linen and gold. Each of those was more than just clothing, but a symbol of his position and perceived value to society.

Sometime between getting the impressive coat from his father and getting the luxurious robes from Pharaoh, Joseph learned not to base his identity on things like his clothes, circumstances, or reputation. He has been a pampered son, a slave, a prisoner, and a prime minister. He has endured the jealousy of his brothers, the lust and lies of Potiphar's wife, and the dreams of Pharaoh. The only thing they all have in common is that we repeatedly read God was with him, and he prospered in whatever he did. Bitterness and unforgiveness tie us to the past and blind us to God's goodness in the present. Joseph instead found his true identity as a servant of God in every situation. Circumstances will always change, but God never does.

Against All Odds

Exodus 2-14

Aburning bush sent some random guy to tell Pharaoh, "Let my people go!" After some strange plagues, he finally did, and they left... right through the middle of the Red Sea! If you know any Bible stories at all, you probably know Moses. Only Jesus himself is more prominent in a typical children's Bible. Moses is a remarkable case study of the simple principle, "listen to God and do what He says." Sometimes he got that right and was able to be at the center of extraordinary works of God that we marvel at 4000 years later. Other times, Moses messed it up in some spectacular ways and seemingly derailed the fate of his entire nation. Let's look at a few examples.

Moses is anything but some random guy in the desert. He is born a slave. His people, the nation of Israel, also known as Hebrews, are slaves in Egypt. The king, aka

Pharaoh, recently enacted some population control and ordered that every baby boy be thrown in the river (i.e., to drown). We read right past that bit because it's just setting the scene for one of the famous Moses stories, but let that sink in for a moment. Scholars estimate their population at the time to be roughly the same as the entire city of Houston, Texas. Every baby boy in an area that size is taken from his parents and murdered at birth. No doubt, any parents who resist the order are executed themselves. So, when Moses's mother hides her baby for three months to keep him alive, she does so at the risk of her own life and potentially the whole family.

I don't know how or where you conceal a newborn baby in slave housing that doesn't have much privacy in general, but her technique only works for a few months. Next, she gets creative and builds a little boat out of a basket to float him down the river, hoping God will somehow take care of him. It looks crazy to us, but this technically obeys the law by putting him in the river while still giving him at least a tiny chance of survival. She is hoping against hope at this point, and it works! The king's daughter comes to bathe downstream—we don't know how far downstream, maybe Moses floats for miles—but she spots the basket, finds the baby inside, feels pity, and adopts him. I wonder how that conversation goes down when she tells her dad, who ordered the execution of all these babies, that she decided to keep one. Daddy's little girl apparently gets her way because she raises Moses as a prince of Egypt. Does that end the whole law too? Nothing tells us how long that order lasts, but since Moses isn't the only male in his generation, the boys are allowed to live again at some point.

The Bible never tells us how or when Moses learns of his true heritage. Maybe Egyptians and Israelites look so different that it's obvious. Perhaps he grows up hearing the story of how they found him in the river (that seems likely since his name means "pulled out" because she pulled him out of the water). Maybe it's even a life-altering revelation that he learns as an adult. Whatever the case, adult Moses knows he is an Israelite like the slaves he sees daily. He apparently also knows the prophecy that God will rescue them from slavery because he connects the dots and realizes his unique potential to pull that off.

When he spots an Egyptian beating a Hebrew slave, he intervenes and kills the Egyptian. That slave clearly talks about it because the very next day, Moses discovers people already know the story. News soon reaches the king, who essentially signs Moses's death warrant. Moses flees the country, undoubtedly convinced that he screwed everything up. He ruined at least his own life, not to mention blowing his entire nation's chance of escaping slavery. Can you imagine how that would mess with your head? Have you ever been deeply disappointed when something you tried didn't work out, so you just wanted to spend some time alone? I think that is why he spends a full third of his life living in the middle of nowhere and working as a shepherd. That is about as far away from everyone and everything as possible. He spends the bulk of his time—possibly for days or weeks at a time—alone in the wilderness with no one but sheep. We only get a few sentences about these 40 years, but I think we can fairly call it wallowing in his misery.

One day he spots a bush on fire. The text makes it sound like that wasn't particularly unusual because the fire isn't what catches his attention, but rather the fact that the bush isn't burning away. When he looks closer at the mystery bush, it talks to him! I think this story is hilarious. We treat it like this epic event because people have made movies about it, but this is still an 80-year-old guy alone in the wilderness talking to a bush! Moses is so broken from his jumping-the-gun failure that, even when God announces Himself and His plan, he tries to miss this opportunity.

When God first tells him to rescue Israel, Moses says, "Who am I to try that?" Don't forget, he's a nobody here, and a failure and fugitive in Egypt. God says, "I'll be with you," so Moses effectively says, "Well then, who are you?" I imagine him thinking, "*Oh good, the bush will help me. 'Hey Pharaoh, I found a bush out in the desert that's really upset with you. You should totally give up free labor and let all your slaves go worship the bush with me.'*" God declares His name and says the Israelites will listen to Moses while Pharaoh won't. That makes Moses's response a little strange. "What if they don't believe me?" At this point, God gives him a few miracles to perform at will to prove his credibility. Moses can tell this debate isn't going his way, so he tries a different tactic. "I'm not so good at the whole talking-and-words-coming-out-good thing. And based on how I'm currently losing an argument with a *bush*, it doesn't look like 'your presence' has made me any better at it." God is either fed up or laughing at this point, it's hard to tell, but He essentially says, "I made your mouth in the first place. Stop arguing with me and just go!" Moses runs out of excuses and begs, "Please send someone else."

Those movies I mentioned only exist because he eventually returns to Egypt and confronts Pharaoh. Here is where it gets good. Moses starts with those couple of little parlor tricks God taught him at the bush, but Pharaoh is unimpressed. God cranks things up a notch and dives into what most of us know as the plagues of Egypt. You might not realize how each one is a direct insult to Egyptian gods and goddesses. From the Nile River to animals to weather, every plague has at least one deity that it completely mocks.

- Oh, you have a frog god? Have an infestation of frogs.
- You have a god of healing? Here's a terrible skin disease that your celebrated Egyptian medicine can't touch.
- You worship the sun? Try total darkness for three days.

You can Google it yourself if you want to dig into the whole list, but this is no random assortment of magic tricks. God declared upfront (in Exodus 7) that He would prove to all of Egypt that He is the only true God who reigns over everything. This is show and tell.

Moses looks like a god to the Egyptians, performing these outrageous miracles. That is especially impressive for someone who presumably grew up in this very palace. Moses previously thought his position in Pharaoh's household qualified him to rescue the Israelites. Then he ran for his life, hid in the desert for 40 years, and didn't even want to return. Here he stands, putting on the most remarkable exhibition in history, seemingly impervious to any threat from Pharaoh or anyone else. What made such a change in this man? The difference is that this time he is following God's instructions. We can't even call it completely voluntary because he tried his best to get out of it. Still, once he gets started and sees the power of God with his own eyes, nothing else can intimidate him.

It isn't the last time God works miracles through Moses. He will soon lead these people on a path through the Red Sea. He learned it the hard way, but Moses now recognizes that he is not exceptional. His background and education accomplished nothing, but things work out when he simply listens to God and does what He says. Sure, it might look crazy at the time, but God knows what He's doing and always gets the job done. He could surely do it without Moses if He wanted to, but He chooses to work through people, even if it takes 80 years to get them ready for it. What could He do through you if you just listened to God and did what He said?

Logic Is Optional

Joshua 3-6

Joshua gets my vote for the most underrated guy in the entire Bible. I'm talking about Moses's successor (no pressure there!), who led an unruly band of desert wanderers in one of the most amazing conquests the world has ever known. And yet, the most we can usually say about him is, "Joshua fought the battle of Jericho, and the walls came tumbling down." If you spent your childhood in Sunday School and VBS like me, you can't say that without singing it. I can't decide if that makes it better or worse.

Before we get to that most famous battle, let's see who this guy is. Joshua enters the narrative as Moses's assistant sometime after the Israelites cross the Red Sea. We don't know much about what he does during that time, but we can assume he has a front-row seat to Moses's best and worst moments. He undoubtedly learns some great lessons along the way:

+ The value of trusting God in any and all circumstances
+ How to lead people who don't always want to follow you
+ How to move forward when you screw up

I'm sure there were dozens more throughout a 40-year apprenticeship under one of the most revered leaders in world history. That's worth something.

When the day comes that Moses dies and Joshua officially takes his place as the leader of this fickle group, he leads the next generation. Rather than a pack of former slaves, Joshua gets to lead a group that grew up wandering in the wilderness. Few still remember the old slavery, God's plagues to free them, or even crossing the Red Sea. To many of them, those are merely stories their parents and grandparents used to tell them— *true* stories, but stories nonetheless. Joshua must lead this group into the Promised Land. You know, the land currently inhabited by established kingdoms in fortified cities, and at least some of them are giants. How hard could that be?

The first step is simply getting there. That will be a challenge because it means crossing the Jordan River, which is currently at flood stage. Sensible leadership would say to wait a month or two until the river settles back down. They already spent 40 years in the wilderness, what's a couple more months? But God wants to use Joshua and the land of Canaan to make a point here, just like He did with Moses and Egypt.

How do you get a million or so people herding their livestock and carrying everything they own across a swollen river? By trusting God to get you across. Moses only had to wave his hand over the Red Sea and watch it part for them to cross. Joshua is not so lucky. He has to send the priests, carrying the Ark of the Covenant, out into the raging river, based on God's promise that He'll stop the river when they get out there. The Bible never clearly says how many people it takes to carry the Ark, but a handful of guys must walk directly into a flooded river carrying a top-heavy burden. Of course, God does what He said, and it works. The waters *stand in one heap* upstream, whatever that means. I would love to see how that looks! The entire nation crosses on dry ground, much to the dismay of the nearby cities that see these people miraculously invading their land.

Now is the perfect time to strike, with the locals terrified by the mystical powers of these desert wanderers. Yet again, God thinks differently. Before He can give them the Promised Land, they must restore His covenant with them. Joshua gets the delightful job of circumcising all the men because they hadn't done it to the babies born in the desert. Whether or not he performs that job with his own hands, he at least has to convince thousands of grown men to go through it. Let's just say it's easier with a baby who doesn't get a vote. But Joshua must have learned some exceptional leadership lessons from Moses because this seemingly gets done without any problem. That mass surgery leaves them sitting awkwardly in Canaanite territory, completely defenseless, with all of the able-bodied fighting men too tender to fend off any attack. In Genesis 34, a couple of their patriarchs took advantage of that same healing process to slaughter an entire town. You can bet that everyone knows that story and recognizes the similarities. This is a significant move of utter dependence upon God because He is the only thing protecting them from being completely wiped out.

Once everyone heals enough to fight again (I understand it generally takes a couple of weeks), Joshua shares the battle plan that God gave him. It sounds as ridiculous as His river-crossing plan. Once again, the Ark goes first, and the whole army will follow. Instead of crossing a river, they will march a lap around the biggest, strongest city without saying a word, then return to camp. They'll put on this little parade for the inhabitants of Jericho every day for a week. Then on the seventh day, they'll walk seven laps instead of just one (still not saying anything the whole time). When the priests blow some horns at the end of the last lap, everyone will shout to God, and the city will collapse. Makes perfect sense, right?

Once again, I am most impressed by Joshua's ability to convince the people to go along with this. It makes no sense, it has never happened in the history of the world, and no one in their right mind would expect it to work. Then again, they just saw what God did to the floodwaters of the Jordan, and He protected them while they were healing from circumcision. Joshua has never led them wrong, so they go for it. I could understand a charismatic leader rallying the people for the first day, maybe even a second day. But a whole week of marching in ranks around the enemy city has to make people wonder if this will ever work. They did not talk during their little parade, but you can be sure a lot of questioning and grumbling occurred once they returned to camp. But there is no plan B, so they keep going. Sure enough, when they finish the seventh lap on the seventh day (God likes sevens) and blow the horns and shout, the wall falls flat. The army rushes right in and utterly destroys the city.

Not exactly a shock that skeptics doubt this story. The funny thing is archaeologists have studied the ruins of Jericho. I once saw a documentary showing how the evidence proves the walls were not destroyed by a sonic blast, as though that disproved the Bible. The unique thing is that the wall of Jericho fell outward, which doesn't happen from a conquering army or even an earthquake. Archaeology cannot explain that. But God said the wall would fall flat, so it did.

My favorite part of that documentary was where they looked at the other cities in the region (which the Israelites gradually conquered) and insisted that no invading army destroyed them. They claimed it was more likely a series of massive earthquakes. These Israelites allegedly were not mighty warriors but simple nomads who wandered into the ruins of a city after a natural disaster and claimed it for themselves. I see it a bit differently.

God promised in Deuteronomy 2:25 that He would make everyone fear the Israelite army. Before they even crossed the Jordan, Rahab told the spies in chapter 2 that everyone was terrified of them. How much do you suppose Jericho's supernatural defeat freaked out the neighboring kingdoms? Israel then marches through the land, conquering one nation after another. Science now tells us the fortified cities were devastated by earthquakes! As far as the locals can tell, this army can dry up rivers to cross and shake the very ground to destroy your defenses. That would surely make everyone fear the Israelite army!

I suppose it boils down to confirmation bias, which means you will see what you expect to see. Skeptics interpret the evidence to show they were opportunistic scavengers instead of conquerors. To me, the very same evidence proves the story that God was fighting for them and giving them the land.

In the end, Joshua's leadership always amazes me. He trusted God and followed His directions even when they seemed absurd. Most impressively, he convinced a ragtag generation of nomads with a track record of more complaining than fighting to go along with it. God means what He says, and even the parts that don't align with our logic are sacred promises He cannot and will not break. You can trust Him just like Joshua did. Who knows? Maybe He'll guide you to do things as astonishing as Joshua did.

Worst. Haircut. Ever.

Judges 13:2-7; 14; 15:9-17; 16+

God once gave some random guy massive strength as long as he didn't cut his hair. He acted like a superhero until he fell for a woman who secretly cut his hair off and made him weak. The life of Samson sounds like it belongs in a comic book more than in the Bible, especially the way we usually remember it. Consequently, it's no shock that skeptics like to use it to question the validity of the Scriptures. Any book that claims such an obvious fairy tale as legitimate history surely can't be trusted, can it?

Samson might not be such an easy target if we paid attention to the whole story instead of just telling the highlights. An angel announces his birth and declares his mission before his mother's pregnancy. Only a handful of people in all of Scripture get that kind of introduction. Samson's prophecy comes with conditions; he will be a Nazirite from birth. That might not mean much to the average American, but the Nazirite vow is a special dedication of your life to God. People usually commit to it for a set time, but this will be Samson's entire life, and he doesn't even get a vote. A Nazirite is pretty much defined by what you cannot do:

- Drink wine or strong drink (aka alcohol)
- Eat anything from the vine (aka grapes or raisins)
- Eat anything unclean (strictly Kosher food)
- Go near a dead body (can't even attend a close relative's funeral)
- Cut your hair until the vow is over (for Samson, that means never)

For some silly reason, we thoroughly gloss over everything but the hair. We ignore the idea of a Nazirite vow and Samson's life entirely dedicated to God and only remember his hair. That vow is essential for the rest of the story because Samson's first remarkable act is killing a lion with his bare hands. I'm pretty sure that counts as touching a dead body. Even if you cut him some slack by calling it self-defense, he comes back several days later to look at the remains, deliberately approaching a dead body. Samson goes a step further when he discovers some bees living in the dead lion (is that a thing bees do?) and eats some of their honey. This undoubtedly violates the dead body rule, and that honey you scooped out of a lion carcass surely qualifies as unclean food. He already broke two out of five rules. And by the way, this whole lion thing happens on his way to a nearby town to fetch the woman he wants to marry. Samson seems unconcerned that she is a pagan woman and, therefore, technically off-limits according to God. That's not specifically part of the Nazirite vow, but Samson certainly doesn't appear very dedicated to God. When he arrives for the wedding with his pagan bride, he throws a feast for the locals. The word "feast" here literally means "drinking," so it's a safe bet that Samson also violates the no alcohol rule.

That marriage ends badly. Samson makes a bet with the locals over a riddle he made up about the lion he killed, which is wildly unfair because they could not possibly know that. They threaten Samson's wife, who nags him relentlessly until he finally tells her the answer. He gets furious when he loses the bet because she shared the secret. As in, kills-30-people-and-leaves furious. When he eventually calms down and comes back for his wife, he finds her already married to someone else. In response, he pretty much wages a one-man war against the Philistines.

We have reached the superhero part of the story, where his supernatural strength comes into play. He snaps the ropes they use to bind him. He slaughters a thousand soldiers armed only with the jawbone of a donkey. He carries away the gates of a city (essentially stripping them of their defenses) with his bare hands. In a word, Samson is unstoppable. At least until he falls for another woman, that is.

We tend to assume Samson and Delilah have a shallow, purely physical relationship, but the text doesn't tell us that. It explicitly says that Samson loves this woman, and her effect on him makes that seem pretty accurate. There is less evidence that she loves him back. Delilah is a Philistine, and her rulers offer to pay her handsomely to uncover the secret of Samson's strength. She at once takes the deal and starts working on him.

Here we see the biggest issue with how we remember Samson's story. We always picture him as some muscle-bound hulk with long flowing hair. That might make sense because he is strong and never cuts his hair, but why are the Philistine leaders desperate to find the secret of his great strength? There wouldn't be much of a secret if he were some giant bodybuilder type. No one would pay Delilah to figure out why the dude with enormous muscles is so strong. I suspect he is a normal-looking guy who happens to be inexplicably strong. That's the mystery they are so eager to solve.

Either that or Samson has more than just strength, and he is more like an actual comic book superhero that no one can kill. There *was* that time he single-handedly fought an army and killed a thousand armed soldiers with a bone he found lying around. Are you telling me not a single one of those soldiers even landed a hit on him? Nobody had a spear or arrows or even the sense to attack from behind while he fought somebody else? Perhaps Samson's great strength goes beyond his ability to lift heavy things. It makes no difference for the story, but it's fun to ponder.

A woman nagging Samson to reveal a secret is nothing new. He should remember how many problems resulted from the last time he gave in. He would flatly refuse if he learned from the past. He would tell her the truth if he loved her and believed she would never betray his trust. Instead, he toys with her. She explicitly asks how he can be bound and subdued, which ought to be a warning sign. She immediately tries the fake answer he gives, which should be even more of a red flag. Rather than heed the warning, Samson continues. This cycle happens two more times: he gives a fake answer, she immediately tries it to no avail, and instead of Samson leaving the toxic situation, Delilah gets mad at him for tricking her, and he keeps going.

Here we see Samson's fatal flaw. I'm not sure if it is a weakness for women, overconfidence in himself, or if he is just... not smart. Whatever the case, he does not learn. He eventually caves and tells her about the Nazirite vow, or at least part of it. Samson seemingly forgets the rest of the rules for a Nazirite and reports that shaving his head would make him like any other man. Delilah recognizes at once this is finally the honest answer. She calls the Philistine lords to set an ambush, gets Samson to fall asleep, and has a man secretly shave his head. When the Philistines attack, his strength is gone, and they take him prisoner.

Samson's story is not over quite yet. The Philistines, of course, feel the need to celebrate their victory over Samson. When they're all good and drunk, they decide to bring him in to gloat over him. They gouged out his eyes when they captured him, so now he needs to be led by the hand. He stands with his hands resting on the main pillars supporting the temple and prays for God to strengthen him one last time. Significantly, this is the only prayer we know of Samson ever saying (unless you count the time he complained to God because fighting made him thirsty). True to his character, Samson mainly asks for revenge, a recurring theme in his life. God evidently grants the request because Samson knocks down the building with all of the Philistine lords in it and kills more people in his death than he did in the rest of his life.

So, was the strength really in his hair? Samson clearly thought so, as do most people to this day. The Bible even mentions that although they finally defeated him by shaving his head, the Philistines let his hair grow back by the end. I would have shaved his head daily to play it safe. But I believe his strength had less to do with his hair than the Nazirite vow: the total dedication of his life unto God. As callously as he violated the other restrictions, he *considered* himself a Nazirite as long as he never cut his hair. When he completely breaks that vow, we see the saddest line in all of Scripture, *"he did not know that the Lord had left him."* (Judges 16:20) His strength returns when he finally prays and acknowledges that it was never in himself but from God.

The shocking part is that God honored Samson's interpretation of a Nazirite. By the letter of the law, Samson violated his vow long before he told Delilah, *"I was dedicated to God as a Nazirite from birth."* (16:17

NLT) He still considered himself a Nazirite with his life specially dedicated to God. The hair was just the last straw of completely breaking his vow. In the end, even though he appears more concerned with vengeance than rededicating his life, God again meets him where he is and empowers Samson.

I see this as the most critical lesson from Samson's life. You don't need to be perfect or have everything straightened out to be used by God.

- Even if you repeatedly get wrapped up in bad relationships and compromise your convictions...
- Even if you constantly make the same mistakes without learning from them...
- Even if you're not very bright...
- Even if you get a terrible haircut...

...God can meet you where you are and accomplish great things through you.

Who Is This Guy?

When an actual event becomes such a common metaphor that people who don't even know the story refer to it by name, you know this was a significant day. "David and Goliath" became a universal term for any situation where the little guy takes on something way out of his league. Unfortunately, many people view it like *The Tortoise and the Hare*, nothing more than a fable to inspire the underdog. For starters, I'm reasonably confident no tortoise ever really challenged a hare to a footrace. David and Goliath were actual people who actually fought on an actual field of battle to decide the fate of actual armies. More importantly, this conflict has so much more than an unexpected victory.

We generally remember the story as a small shepherd boy killing a giant soldier with a sling. The problem for Americans like me is we picture Dennis the Menace

71

with a slingshot in his back pocket, which isn't even close. David is a youth in this passage, but that only means he is too young to join the army, which makes him less than twenty. Since he is also sent alone to the front lines with a care package for his brothers, I doubt we're talking about a six or seven-year-old child. He's probably a teenager. Teenage boys are notorious for behaving like they're invincible, so taking on this giant would fit that pattern.

More importantly, the sling is no child's toy; it was the artillery of that day. Skilled slingers could hit a bird in flight, and Judges 20:16 tells of some who could hit a hair. Far from tiny pebbles, they threw stones the size of golf balls or larger. The preferred ammunition in that particular region was an abnormally dense and heavy rock. An experienced thrower (it's more about technique than strength) could hurl them well over 300 miles per hour. Without going into a detailed lesson on ballistics, let's just say that these stones hit with the approximate force and accuracy of at least a musket. An exceptionally talented slinger probably makes it more like a modern rifle. While it doesn't quite equal the range of firearms, a sling is still a long-distance projectile weapon in a world where armies mostly fight with swords and spears. Generals often used slingers against armored infantry.

David arrives at the scene while Goliath stands on the opposite hill shouting his challenge for representative combat. Opposing armies commonly choose a champion from each side and have the two fight to the death. The winner of that combat decides the battle instead of the entire army fighting and more people dying. Unsurprisingly, no one in Israel's army wants to fight a giant. Scholars have argued over Goliath's size for centuries, with estimates ranging from seven to thirteen feet tall. Regardless of the actual numbers, we know he towers over the Israelites, sufficiently intimidating them. At least until a teenage boy with some profound fighting experience (more on that later) hates seeing the entire army cower from a big bully with a sword. He blurts out something along the lines of, "For crying out loud, I could take this guy out."

David's eagerness to take on Goliath soon finds him standing before the king, explaining himself. Don't miss the irony here. The Bible describes King Saul as standing head and shoulders above everyone else, so he is quite possibly their most intimidating warrior. Regardless of height, he's unquestionably their king and leader, making him the obvious choice to answer

Goliath's challenge. David makes it worse by recounting his personal history of fighting off lions and bears as a shepherd, which is more significant than you might think. For starters, the text never mentions him using a sling for that. Maybe he had a club or something, but it sounds like he just killed them with his bare hands. The less obvious part is the size of an adult lion or bear falls in that same range as Goliath's height. While everyone else just sees how much bigger he is than the other soldiers, David sees him as about the same as those fierce animals he already killed. He confidently says that God gave him victory back then, and He will surely do it now.

I don't know if this offends Saul, but it should at least embarrass him. He is God's anointed king, chosen to lead the army in battle. He should boldly face this enemy, confident that God will give him victory. Instead, he hides in his tent, looking at an underage boy who can't wait to do the job. Eventually, Saul agrees and sends David. Nothing in the text quite explains why. Maybe David's confidence that God will hand Goliath over to him or something? Saul tries to put his armor on David, which of course, doesn't fit (remember how tall Saul is?), and David rejects it because he's not used to that kind of equipment. He walks out to the battle-field with the gear he knows, a shepherd's staff and his sling, stopping at a stream to gather a few good stones. I like that he takes more than one. David trusts God for victory but doesn't assume it will be easy.

More importantly, the text plainly says that he carries *his* staff and *his* sling. That's how we know that David probably was one of those skilled slingers I described earlier, even though the Bible never mentions him using a sling before or after this day. If he brought his sling along on an errand to deliver food to his brothers, odds are he always carried it with him. It was part of his identity, like that shepherd's staff. Go back to what we know about teenage boys in general. That kid who always has a football on hand tends to be pretty good at football. The guy you never see without his skateboard is darn good at skateboarding. And you can bet that the one who always has his sling with him knows how to use it effectively.

Goliath gets offended when he sees David approaching. Here he stands, the mighty Philistine champion, a heavily armed giant, and they send a boy with a stick to fight him. He taunts and curses David. David says Goliath is not fighting a boy or even the army of Israel, but against God. That might sound like David's own taunt, but I see it more like a final warning. Goliath steps forward to fight, evidently not intimidated by Israel's God, so David charges in and quickly takes a shot with his sling. The Bible says that stone literally sinks into Goliath's forehead, and he falls on his face dead. No one realized until that moment that Goliath had brought a knife to a gunfight. David had him completely outclassed!

David uses Goliath's sword to cut off his head. This matters for a few reasons. Firstly, both armies are standing at a distance, so a severed head unquestionably proves that Goliath is dead and the battle is over. David promised to cut off Goliath's head but carried no sword of his own, so he had to use the giant's sword to do it. The funny part is that the sword is probably nearly as big as David. Even Goliath's head would be conspicuously large compared to the shepherd boy who picks it up. In a dark twist, David carries that head around with him for the rest of the day like some sort of trophy and brings it clear back to Jerusalem. No idea what becomes of it after that...

We generally tell this story as though this is just David's personality. He's the kid who fights off lions and bears with his bare hands when they try to steal his sheep, so he's not intimidated by a man in armor. But if you look at David's words, he focuses entirely on God's power. He doesn't brag about the beasts he killed; they were just examples of God's deliverance. Why should this fight be any different? More importantly, David is not some random kid. Sometime before this day, he was anointed as the future king. It was pretty secretive, so not many people know about it yet, and David has the sense not to bring it up while talking to Saul, the current king. Still, I suspect much of his confidence comes from knowing that he already has God's promise over his life. Even his final warning to Goliath clarifies that David isn't counting on his combat skills. *"You come to me with a sword and with a spear and with a javelin, but I come to you in the name of the Lord of hosts, the God of the armies of Israel, whom you have defied... the Lord will deliver you into my hands... that all this assembly may know that the Lord saves not with sword and spear. For the battle is the Lord's, and He will give you into our hand."* (1 Samuel 17:45-47)

That's a big deal because it means David is no different from us. I don't know about you, but I definitely never killed an angry bear with my bare hands. And I'm not very eager to square off against an oversized trained soldier either. What made David special wasn't his track record of fighting wild animals but his willingness to trust God, regardless of who or what he was facing. David didn't even have the advantage of the Holy Spirit living inside of him like we do if we follow Jesus. David didn't have promises like James 4:7-8, *"Resist the devil, and he will flee from you. Draw near to God, and he will draw near to you."* Even without some of our advantages, David struck down a giant and rescued his country from slavery. What victories might God win in our lives if we just step up and give Him a chance?

What Really Matters?

1 Kings 18-19

Of all the stories I remember hearing in Sunday School as a child, I think my favorite was Elijah calling down fire from Heaven. It always sounded awesome, and I can still picture the illustration from my old children's Bible. It's just one of those things that makes you wish you could have been there to see it. Today we have intellectual debates about God's existence and people insisting that all faiths are equally valid. Couldn't God just make some epic display of power like that and settle it once and for all? Let's look at the story and see what it's all about.

Elijah steps onto the scene out of nowhere and announces a drought without so much as saying why. I can understand King Ahab's frustration when he finally sees Elijah again, three years into this drought. Elijah blames everything on Ahab for turning his back on God and worshiping Baal, so he arranges a public showdown to figure out which god is worth worshiping. Elijah lays it all on the line, telling the people to stop wavering from one god to another and finally pick one. *"If the Lord is God, follow Him; but if Baal, then follow him."* (1 Kings 18:21) That seems pretty reasonable to me.

Elijah, the lone prophet of God, faces off against 450 prophets of Baal. Each side will prepare an altar with a sacrifice but not light the fire. Whichever God can light the fire to burn the sacrifice will be the winner. Everyone agrees with the terms. I like the absence of criteria for what to do if both fires light. Both sides assume they are the only correct one, and the other team is deluded. The people must be equally convinced that they could not *both* be gods, but they cannot decide which one is real.

Elijah has the distinct advantage of serving the Living God, who cannot possibly lose this contest, so he makes a game of it. He lets Baal's team go first, prepping their sacrifice and calling on Baal all morning with no response. Around noon, Elijah takes it up a notch and starts making fun of them, telling them they should probably scream a little louder. He suggests Baal might be distracted, busy pooping (yes, he says that), out of town, or asleep. This goes on for a few more hours, so I'm sure that's just some highlights of Elijah's taunts. The prophets go all out trying to summon Baal to answer them: dancing, praying, screaming, and ritually cutting themselves. Nothing works. Nothing happens.

As evening approaches, Elijah calmly rebuilds a ruined altar of God. He calls the people to himself and prepares his sacrifice. Seemingly dissatisfied with the current weirdness level of this day, he digs a trench around the altar and says to dump jugs of water over it. They do it three times until it soaks the entire altar and fills the trench. What is he doing here? Perhaps just making sure the wood is wet so no one can claim he cheated? Only God can light a fire in these conditions.

I believe there's more to it than that because this is the only time in the entire Bible that anyone douses an altar with water. That was never part of the instructions for sacrifices. This event takes place at the top of Mount Carmel, meaning some poor guys have to travel at least partway down the mountain to fill jugs of water and carry them back up to dump them. Elijah makes them take three trips. Also, they are three years into a severe drought. Water is precious at this point and he has them dump twelve jugs over this altar. *Maybe* they could use salt water, but the sea is a three-hour walk from here, so I doubt it. And I don't think you would dump dirty, undrinkable water on God's altar, so this is probably a very costly sacrifice.

Don't forget, Elijah is working solo here. Unlike Baal's prophets, he has no team of people with him, so who does he send for water? It seems to be the people, the citizens of Israel, whom Elijah is calling back to God. Beyond showing them that the God who delivered them from Egypt is the only true God, he draws them into an act of worship. They give up water, which is a big deal for them. Scholars disagree whether the people contribute from their meager rations of drinking water or put time and effort into carrying jugs up the mountain. Either way, they take part in this sacrifice.

When everything is ready, Elijah has no elaborate rituals. He says a short prayer that amounts to, "God, show 'em!" Then fire falls from Heaven. I don't know what that looks like, but it must be epic. This fire doesn't just light the wet wood; it consumes everything—and I mean everything! The bull, the wood, the water, and even the altar's stones are all burned up. The scientific side of my brain wants to call the fire falling a massive lightning strike or maybe even a meteor, but an impact of that magnitude should utterly obliterate Elijah and the gathered crowd. This is just God showing off in a way that modern science can't quite quantify.

Not surprisingly, that makes an impression on everyone who sees it. They at once declare the Lord is God, which is fair because he undoubtedly won the contest. As impressive as that victory is, it barely makes a difference in the overall story. Neither the king nor the crowd is said to change their lives to serve God as a result. One commentary pointed out that the people were *convinced* but not *converted*. All Elijah gets for his victory is a death threat. He retreats to the wilderness, where God confronts him. Elijah complains that everyone has forsaken God, insisting that he's the only one left, and now they want to kill him too. Elijah assumed (as would we all) that when God showed off, it would settle the issue once and for all, but it looks like things have only gotten worse.

God gives Elijah an object lesson that just because something is massive doesn't mean it matters. First, a violent wind blows through, so strong that it rips rocks apart on the mountain, but God is not in the wind. Then a terrible earthquake shakes the entire mountain, but God is not in the earthquake. Then a raging fire tears across the mountain, but God is not in the fire. After three awe-inspiring demonstrations of power, God softly whispers to Elijah that things are not as bleak as he thinks. Still, the real lesson here is not in what that soft voice tells him.

This is all about what truly matters. God's presence is the only thing that can change a person's heart. Even when a sign undeniably comes from God, it does not automatically mean God is in it. The wind, earthquake, and fire are all signs from God, but His presence is not in any of them. None of those stunning displays of power are any help to Elijah, but the gentle whisper assures him that he is not as alone as he feels.

That's important news because he still has work to do. Elijah finally understands that great displays of power can be epic but still empty. Signs and wonders can attract much attention, but they accomplish nothing until you recognize God's presence and hear His voice. From this moment on, nothing seems to impress Elijah anymore. When even a massive display of undeniable evidence didn't quiet the opposition, Elijah felt hopeless until God's still, small voice showed him a different perspective.

The rest of Elijah's life is a lesson in not taking the things of this world too seriously. When he finds an apprentice to carry on his work, Elijah puts a cloak on him and keeps walking. He calmly announces God's judgment on the king, and you can almost hear him yawning as he repeatedly calls more fire from Heaven to kill the troops that come to arrest him for it. He is even remarkably casual when he knows God is about to take him to Heaven.

From the moment he walked onto the scene, Elijah recognized the power and authority of God. He went from one of the most amazing spectacles God has ever performed to such deep despair that he begged God to take his life. Everything changed when God showed him a bigger picture. We need the same thing today. We quickly get so caught up in temporary circumstances that we become shortsighted. Our problems look so big and overwhelming that we naturally want God to show up in powerful ways to counter them. What we need most is the presence of God in our lives. We need to listen to His whisper. Our highest highs and lowest lows in life are equally trivial in light of the glory and majesty of God. If your life is in His hands, nothing else really matters.

Travelling Preacher

Jonah (the whole book)

Jonah got swallowed by a whale and had to build a fire to make it sneeze so he could escape. No, wait, that's Geppetto. Jonah realized he could speak to the whale, and it told him to let go, and it launched him out the blowhole right where he needed to go. No, that was Dory. Well then, what is Jonah's story, and why should we believe it any more than Disney movies?

Jonah is a unique prophet because he does not want to be a prophet. He does not want to speak for God. We don't know Jonah's existing track record as a prophet before God tells him to go to Nineveh. We do know he rejects this mission and flees as far as possible in the opposite direction. Can we acknowledge how silly this is? If Jonah knows anything about God, he surely knows that there is no such thing as escaping His presence. No matter how far he travels, God will be there too. What is Jonah's plan here? He boards a ship to Tarshish–basically the farthest point of the known world–but what will he do once he gets there?

Of course, none of that matters because Jonah never makes it to Tarshish. God sends a massive storm, and the sea is so violent that a pack of seasoned sailors freak out and pray to their various gods. They yell at Jonah for sleeping instead of panicking and praying. Jonah takes responsibility for the storm because he's running from God and says they should throw him overboard. In only twelve verses, this is the second sign that Jonah does not understand God's nature. It won't be the last. First, he tried to run away from Him. Now he thinks that God wants to kill him (and can't get the job done?), and the best way to save everyone else on the boat is to have them essentially murder him by throwing him into the raging sea.

Jonah's announcement only terrifies the sailors more, and they try desperately to save themselves, but it proves hopeless. These men are not worshipers of the true God, but they already fear him based on the fury of this storm. They beg God in advance to forgive them for killing Jonah, then toss him into the sea. The storm stops so suddenly that it freaks them out even more, so they make vows and sacrifices to God. I wish we knew more of their stories. I wonder what effect this day has on the rest of their lives. These details in the Bible imply that those men talked about it enough for it to be known as part of Jonah's story.

Now comes the piece that makes people lose their minds. *"And the Lord appointed a great fish to swallow up Jonah. And Jonah was in the belly of the fish three days and three nights"* (Jonah 1:17). Countless modern intellectuals insist that a person could never survive in the belly of a fish. They usually say "whale" because they don't even pay attention enough to see that God said it's a fish. Much like Noah's Ark, there are plausible explanations for this, but at the end of the day, it doesn't matter. To paraphrase the late great Chuck Smith, would it make you happier if it said God appointed a nuclear submarine to surface and take Jonah on board for three days? God is working a miracle. Why should He be bound by natural laws here any more than when parting a sea, turning a stick into a snake, or making a donkey talk? God is omnipotent, which literally means He can do anything. Whether He chooses to keep Jonah alive inside a fish or on the surface of the sun, terms like "impossible" or even "difficult" simply don't apply to God.

Let's not get all hung up on the fish. It's hardly more than a footnote in the story, mentioned in only three verses. It serves two simple purposes. Firstly, it is a miserable experience for Jonah. He describes the deep darkness and pressure and getting tangled up in seaweed. To me, the most unbelievable part of Jonah's whole story is that it takes three days of this experience before he finally prays to God for deliverance. I feel like three *seconds* would be enough for me. Then again, his description sounds like Jonah assumes he is already in Hell, and it's too late to pray. The second purpose of the fish is plain old transportation. Jonah would surely have drowned in the middle of the sea, but the fish carries him back to land and spits him out. For once, I don't mind the Bible skipping the details!

God repeats His instruction to Jonah, "Get up, go to Nineveh, and deliver my message." Jonah walks into this enormous city and preaches the world's least inspiring sermon: *"40 days from now Nineveh will be destroyed."* (Jonah 3:4 CEV) Maybe there is more to it than that, but that's the message recorded in Scripture. He gives no explanation why destruction is coming, no way of avoiding it, or even anything about Jonah's ordeal getting here. Just, "buckle up, you're all gonna die." It kind of makes you wonder why God was so insistent that Jonah should come to preach this message.

Here is the craziest part of the story. Not the fish, not even the worst sermon ever preached, but what comes after. The first surprise is that the entire city takes God seriously and repents. Regardless of social status, everyone dresses in sackcloth (a sign of mourning and deep distress) and commits to prayer and fasting. The king publicly humbles himself and orders that no one, not even the animals, may eat or drink as everyone prays to God for mercy. Beyond a mere religious ritual, the king's decree publicly commands everyone to turn from their evil ways. Everyone hopes that God *might* spare them, although Jonah gave them no reason to expect it.

True to his character, God forgives them. Jonah, on the other hand, does not. He continues his pattern of not understanding God's nature and gets upset with God for showing mercy. Many people accuse Jonah of racism and hatred towards the people of Nineveh. Even if that is a factor, I think we can afford to cut him a little slack here.

For one thing, why did he need to take the whole trip to come here for God to spare the city? God knew all along how it would end up anyway, and He certainly didn't recruit Jonah for his eloquence. What was the point of the trip for Jonah? If anything, God just turned him into a liar. Jonah boldly declared that God would destroy the city. According to the law, Jonah should be executed as a false prophet when that doesn't happen. I can understand why that might bother him.

The story ends with Jonah mad at God. It always stuck out to me that there is no resolution. Jonah never comes around to seeing it God's way. But much like the story of what the sailors did after throwing Jonah overboard, the only reason we have this story is that Jonah recorded it. He would never have done that if he didn't eventually understand the love of God.

Honestly, I question how well we understand that even now. The text plainly says the people believed God. Centuries earlier, Abraham was declared righteous before God by that same act of faith. Scripture repeatedly highlights that story as the primary example of God's grace and salvation by faith. Even though it's the exact same language for the exact same criteria, we never think of Nineveh becoming just as righteous as Abraham.

I have a theory why not. We have a detailed history of Abraham's godly legacy as the father of the faith, not just spiritually but biologically. Not so with Nineveh. I know no stories of Nineveh becoming a beacon of God's love and mercy in a dark world. We have no records of how any Ninevites lived from that day forward, so we don't trust their repentance. But God did! God, who looks at the heart instead of outward appearance and knows every man's thoughts and motives, saw that they turned from their evil way.

We still do this today, and it makes me furious when I see it. Churches (and Christians) love it when a person has a stirring testimony of God delivering them from a troubled past. We like people who *used to* have a problem, but we're far less receptive to someone who is still working through it. Do you honestly think that everything wrong in Nineveh just disappeared overnight? Of course not! And it doesn't all disappear from a person in an instant, either. It takes time to undo decades of habits and behavioral patterns. But the word "repent" simply means to change your mind. You can switch instantly from seeing it as good to see it as bad. That switch is what counts to God. The moment a person believes God and chooses to turn from their evil way—no matter how long they've gone that way or how evil it was—God instantly counts them as righteous. That is my story. If you have trusted Jesus, that's your story. We're all in the same boat. We are all Nineveh, so let's not act like Jonah, who happily received God's grace himself but didn't think Nineveh deserved it.

Hot and Bothered

Daniel 3

Three guys refuse to obey the king's orders and get thrown into a giant furnace (which the king had ready and waiting for just this purpose??), but they don't burn. The king is so impressed that he congratulates them and worships their God. As we jump into a story that is equal parts impressive and crazy, keep in mind that Daniel unflinchingly records this among the history of King Nebuchadnezzar, a man well-known to history and quite possibly the single most famous person who had ever lived by that time. It would have quickly faded away thousands of years ago if this were merely a cute fable with a happy ending. Let's take a moment to set the scene.

It's roughly 600BC, and Babylon is in the process of literally conquering the world. King Nebuchadnezzar brings the best and brightest from each defeated kingdom to the capital to train and indoctrinate them as Babylonian rulers. Google and Facebook aren't the first juggernauts to deliberately gather the best minds to build their desired future, but Babylon takes it much further and renames the people. Sadly, most of us only know these guys by their slave names: Shadrach, Meshach, and Abednego. These young Hebrew men, probably roughly college age, quickly distinguish themselves as the best of the best and rise to important positions. Then the king has a crazy dream about a statue, which turns out to be a message from God: Nebuchadnezzar is a genuinely remarkable king over a genuinely remarkable kingdom, but it won't last forever because God ultimately controls everything. Nebuchadnezzar is all impressed by the Hebrews and their God... for a little while. Then he decides to build an enormous statue, which looks like a deliberate attempt to defy the dream and insist his kingdom *will* last forever because, you know, he's just that awesome. To drive that point home, he orders that everyone—and he does mean *everyone*—must bow down and worship this statue when they play some special music. Oh, and by the way, they will throw anyone who refuses into a furnace.

Not surprisingly, our Hebrew friends have an issue with that. Some other guys rat them out for not bowing when the music plays, and Nebuchadnezzar flies into a rage. Shockingly, he gives them a second chance. He's not exactly famous for mercy or patience, so these guys must really be exceptional. He is well aware of their devotion to their God, and he doesn't have a problem with it as long as they *also* worship him. But when they take a stand and choose God over and against Nebuchadnezzar, things get... well... heated. He evidently knows their refusal stems from their religion, based on the direct challenge he throws out in verse 15, *"what god will be able to rescue you from my power?"* (NLT)

Their response is honestly the highlight of the whole story, and sadly the children's Bibles rarely include it. Well aware that they're in way over their heads, these boys demonstrate some solid, old-school faith. They boldly tell the most powerful man on Earth that they'd rather be in the fire with God at the center of their lives than out here with him taking God's place. Whether God saves them or not, they're sticking to their guns. We overlook just how impressive that is because we know that they ultimately survive, but they had no idea how it would play out at the time.

Nebuchadnezzar completely loses it and issues the death sentence. True to his over-the-top character, he doesn't just put them in the fire. He orders it heated seven times hotter than usual (how did they check that?) and gets the strongest men in his army to tie them up and throw them in. The flames are so hot that they kill those strong men. I have to wonder what our three heroes are thinking right about now. I imagine they fully expect to die here, but at least with a fire so hot, it should be over quickly, right? Do they regret taking a stand, or are they proud to die for their God? Even if they had hoped for some sort of divine intervention, it's surely too late now. But things take an unexpected turn when the king suddenly freaks out because he sees four men (not three) casually walking around in the fire and calls for them to come out. Shadrach, Meshach, and Abednego walk out of the furnace completely unscathed. The fire doesn't damage their clothes or hair but burns off their bonds. They don't even smell like smoke, and if you've ever been around a campfire or just a cigarette smoker, you know that's a miracle in itself. Nebuchadnezzar is so stunned that he declares their God the "Most High God" and promotes them to even higher positions than before.

Let's take just a minute to consider this fiery furnace. I assume it's a kiln or something, leftover from the construction of this statue. Although, Nebuchadnezzar is a bit crazy and might have deliberately built a giant furnace for no reason but to execute anyone who defied him. It sounds like he included an observation spot where he can watch people burn in his furnace. And I don't know if it has doors or what, but there is a way in and out of it. It says they "fell" into the furnace, which sounds like they got tossed in from the top, but then they freely come out, as though it has an exit. Overall, I suspect the furnace looks much different than it does in most picture Bibles.

What bugs me far more is the glaring omissions from this story. Daniel has this annoying storytelling habit. He gives us zero information from the perspective of the people miraculously protected from violent executions but instead follows the king who witnesses it. We know nothing of what this was like for the three guys in the fire. Was it hot? Could they see or hear each other? Were they just wandering around confused, thinking they must be dead already? The turning point in the whole thing was the fourth guy in the fire with them, and then he is never mentioned again! Bible scholars generally agree that this is an Old Testament appearance of Jesus, and I have no problem with that. Still, the text leaves so many unanswered questions! Did anyone but Nebuchadnezzar even see him? No one else ever mentions him. Why doesn't Nebuchadnezzar call him to come out too? He specifically names the three guys he threw in and then (as far as we can tell) doesn't even ask them about the other guy. He mentions an angel once. That's it.

We too easily overlook a critical detail: God deliberately let them get thrown into the furnace. Many Christians insist God will never put more on you than you can handle, but that is a diabolical lie. He does it all the time! On purpose! He never wanted us to handle things on our own. He would much rather have us recognize how utterly dependent we are on Him.

Countless sermons have been preached from this story because there is so much in it that you can hardly pick which message to emphasize.

- Jesus might not spare you from the worst-case scenario, but He walks with you through it.
- Trusting Jesus even when it looks like all hope is lost gives others a chance to see Him and believe in Him.
- God uses the fires of adversity to burn away what your enemy used to bind you.

These are all excellent lessons worth learning from this story, but did you notice this story is not actually about Shadrach, Meshach, and Abednego? The whole thing is from Nebuchadnezzar's perspective, and we see how it affected him, not the three Hebrew guys. That might be the main point. We all want to be the star of our own stories, but God prefers to use us to impact other people. Jesus is the real main character in everyone's story. Our job is to trust Him no matter how the circumstances look.

These guys knew full well they had no power to resist the king's command. They surely hoped God would intervene, but they decided they would rather suffer *with* God than try to survive *without* him. I think that is the main takeaway here. Following Jesus straight into a fiery furnace is better than walking away from Him to play it safe. Whether He spares us from the fire or not, Jesus is enough.

Slumber Party

Daniel 6

An angry king throws Daniel into a den of lions for reasons, but the lions don't hurt him because of God. This story appears in just about every children's Bible, but I have yet to find an accurate version. Daniel, the king, and especially the lions are all misrepresented, especially in illustrations. Let's try to get a clear picture of this story and see what we can learn from it.

We'll start with Daniel. He was brought to Babylon as a captive slave in his teens or early twenties. Nebuchadnezzar had him castrated, renamed, and indoctrinated with Babylonian religion, government, and philosophy. Safe to say that life has not gone the way Daniel imagined. But the crucial thing about Daniel is that he decided in his heart—long before any of this happened—that he would stay faithful to God, no matter what. He graciously found a way not to eat the food sacrificed to pagan gods. He learned the laws and government of Babylon without adopting their religion or mindset. God gave him great wisdom and understanding, even interpreting dreams for the king on multiple occasions. As a result, Daniel and his friends quickly rose to prominent positions among Babylon's top teachers and advisers.

But this isn't where our story starts. Nebuchadnezzar was long gone when Daniel interpreted another sign for the current king and told him that his kingdom was about to end. That very night, in fact. Daniel was so renowned for his wisdom and sound advice that the conquering nation spared his life. Scholars agree that Daniel was at least in his seventies when the new king, Darius the Mede, kept him as a prominent advisor. By the time our story gets going, he's more like 90. Don't imagine Daniel as a young man in the prime of his life anymore. Picture a wise old man who might not move very fast but can probably answer any question you have.

King Darius sets up a system of governors to oversee his kingdom. He picks three people, including Daniel, to lead the whole thing. Once again, Daniel quickly proves himself far more qualified than anyone else, so Darius plans to make him something like the prime minister. That plan annoys the other guys who decide to get rid of Daniel. Politics apparently haven't changed in thousands of years because their first plan is to run a smear campaign. The only problem is Daniel offers no ammunition. Much to their dismay, he is honest, faithful, and doesn't even make mistakes. Let's acknowledge that for a moment. I want to think I have a pretty good track record, but if someone wanted to dig up dirt on me, I'm sure they could find it. These men have all the resources they could want, but they can find nothing to use against Daniel. The only thing that sticks out about him is his God. He refuses to fall in line with culture and follow their religion.

We might recognize that as Daniel's strength, but they see it as his only weakness. They know that Daniel reveres the king and serves him faithfully, but he will surely choose God if they can force him to choose between his faith and the king. They persuade Darius to make a law that no one can pray to anyone but the king for the next month. That law is ridiculous if you think about it for more than a few seconds. Do you seriously want everyone in your entire kingdom (which is quite large, mind you) to bring their *every* request to you? That will get annoying in a hurry. Darius might not be quite as egotistical as Nebuchadnezzar was, but he falls for it just the same.

Daniel never questions the right thing to do when he learns of the new law. He goes home and prays as usual. The text repeatedly emphasizes that this is his standard routine, just as he has always done, and he doesn't miss a beat over this new law. Daniel is a man of principle. He served at least three pagan kings with such faithfulness that no one could find anything to make him look bad, but when a law tries to stop him from worshiping God, he defies it without flinching. Of course, this is precisely what his enemies hoped to see, and they report him at once.

We see no evidence of Daniel being disturbed in the slightest. Meanwhile, Darius is distraught and spends the entire day searching for a loophole to save him. Since even the king cannot override an official law, he must throw Daniel into the lions' den. Darius puts his royal seal on the stone covering the mouth of the lion's den so that no one can even try to rescue Daniel. Then he spends the night fasting, which might imply prayer, but the Bible never says that Darius follows God. He is too stressed and nervous to sleep and rushes out first thing in the morning to see what happened. He calls out to Daniel, twice emphasizing Daniel's relationship to God and asking if God "was able" to rescue him. Part of me wonders if this is the very reason God saves Daniel. Just imagine God's response to hearing that question. *"Am I able? You have no idea who you're dealing with..."*

Of course, God is able, and Daniel is fine. You should have known that in advance, not just because God is more powerful than a lion, but because Daniel is the one who recorded this story for us, so he obviously lived to tell the tale. That's the most frustrating part of the whole thing to me. Daniel tells this story, but we barely get a hint of what that night was like for him, focusing instead on the king's restless night. All he says is that an angel shut the lions' mouths so they wouldn't hurt him. How did that look? Did the lions suddenly become cuddly kittens who snuggled Daniel all night? Did they keep ferociously trying to attack him while the angel fought them off all night? Or did the angel smack them so hard on the first approach that they spent the rest of the night cowering from Daniel? I would much rather know this story than Darius's. In Daniel's defense, he was in a cave overnight with a stone covering the only opening. It was probably too dark for Daniel to see in any detail.

The official sentence must only require one night in the lion's den because Darius brings him out at first light. The children's Bibles usually leave out the part where they arrest Daniel's accusers (along with their wives and children, by the way) and toss them to the lions, who instantly rip them to shreds. On a brighter note, Darius sends a proclamation to his entire kingdom, which encompasses the whole known world, praising Daniel's God and telling everyone to respect Him. He does not command them to worship God, and the text never explicitly says he does either. Still, Darius understands that God can do anything.

Daniel famously foreshadows Jesus:

- Daniel spent his life as a servant in a foreign land.
  - o Jesus left Heaven and came to Earth as a servant.
- Daniel was faithful to God, and even when his enemies wanted to accuse him, they could find no fault in him except in his relationship with God.
  - o Jesus was faithful to His Father, and His enemies could not accuse Him of anything other than calling God His Father.
- Daniel received a death sentence, spent the night in a lion's den sealed with a stone, and emerged unharmed.

○ Jesus received a death sentence, spent three days and nights in a tomb sealed with a stone, and emerged resurrected to new life.

Both stories hinge on the same question Darius asked, "Is God able to rescue you?" A resounding "YES!" echoes throughout history and right down to this very moment. God is still willing and able to rescue any who calls on Him. Will you?

Family Drama

Luke 2:1-20

I can't speak for the rest of the world, but here in America, we have a pretty universal mental image of the first Christmas. We have remarkably consistent imagery for Christmas cards, pageants, storybooks, and decorations, with precious little of it based on Scripture. At best, it begins loosely based on Scripture before being heavily interpreted through culture and tradition. Have you ever seen a movie based on a book, but then you read the book and realized the film was completely off? It's a lot like that...

Let's start with the main characters. Mary and Joseph are an unusual couple. She is young, probably a teenager, while many scholars think Joseph is significantly older. That much does not make them memorable in their culture of arranged marriages. Mary turns up pregnant somewhere between making that plan and the actual wedding day. That alone isn't unique either, but it gets more unusual when Mary insists that she is still a virgin and that the child she carries is from God Himself. Joseph takes it a step further by believing her story (sure, that took some convincing, but that's another story). They get married, but Mary remains a virgin while Joseph intends to raise a son he knows is not his. We can safely assume that most of their family and friends consider Mary an unfaithful liar and Joseph a fool for staying with her.

Further complicating things, the whim of a far-off emperor forces them to travel to Bethlehem. Here's the first place we go wrong because nearly every picture shows super-pregnant Mary sitting on a donkey while Joseph leads it along. I doubt many pregnant women would enjoy a 90-mile donkey ride. The more common (not to mention more comfortable) way to make the trip would be with the donkey pulling a cart where she can sit. More importantly, the Bible never mentions a donkey. People in other stories sometimes ride around on donkeys, which is usually a status symbol showing that they don't have to walk like the commoners. Based on the sacrifice she brings to the temple a few weeks later, we know Joseph and Mary are poor. I suspect they both walk the whole way. It would be a tedious and exhausting trip with or without a donkey, but when the emperor says to go, you have no choice.

Also, just how pregnant is Mary at this point? The Greek word there literally means "swollen with child," which merely implies that she is showing. We know she spent three months with Elizabeth, so Mary is at least in her second trimester. Yet we always imagine her full term, barely making it to Bethlehem before she goes into labor. The text simply says she gives birth while in Bethlehem, and nothing tells us how long they stay there. The Roman census that prompted this trip would not happen in a single day. How anxious would you be to repeat the grueling journey back home even later in pregnancy? Mary famously gives birth in a stable and puts baby Jesus in a manger because there is no room for them in the inn. The most remarkable event in the history of creation gets a single verse of exposition, Luke 2:7. Even so, there is so much to unpack here. I'll just apologize in advance because not only am I going to completely nerd out here, but I'm about to obliterate your nativity scene.

We have whole stories of Joseph searching the town for a place they could sleep and repeatedly getting turned away because there's no room. Then finally, a kind innkeeper lets them stay in the barn with the animals. The Bible says nothing about any innkeeper. Bethlehem is a backwater town of a few hundred people and certainly not a tourist destination, so there is probably no inn in the sense we think of it. Bear in mind that this culture strongly emphasizes hospitality (see Genesis 19:1-3, Judges 19:14-21). On the rare occasion when travelers come to Bethlehem, they most likely stay in someone's home.

So then, why does Luke mention an inn and a manger? Well, now we have to dig into the culture a bit deeper. Homes in this region follow a fairly standard model with one main room for cooking and eating, visiting and resting, and pretty much everything. For many people, that also includes sleeping, but families with a little more money might have a separate bedroom. There is another room for the animals, much like an attached garage in today's world. This room is not for a whole flock of sheep or anything, but they might have a couple of goats for milk or maybe a donkey. It is just a small stable to keep a few animals in the house. Along with keeping the animals safe, their body heat helps keep the house warm at night. Wealthier families could also have a guest room. Here is where it gets interesting. The animal space is called the manger, and the guest room is called the inn. Some Bible translations don't even say "inn," but rather "guest room" or "guest chambers."

As I said, the Bible only gives us one verse, so our imagery is all speculation, but here's how I picture it. Joseph travels to Bethlehem, his family's ancestral hometown. Odds are he still has family living there, which would be the logical place for him to stay. The family would naturally gather around the oldest living patriarch. Think of it like the whole family traveling to Grandma's house for the holidays. Joseph and Mary probably get there late (which would make sense with Mary in no condition to hurry), and cousins and siblings already claimed all the beds. Or it could be that the family rejects Mary's story and views her as a harlot, so they aren't welcome in the guest room. Some translations say there was no *place* for them in the inn, which doesn't necessarily mean no *room*.

Whether from a lack of space or acceptance, their only choice is the attached stable. Here is where Mary gives birth... maybe. The Bible says that she *laid* him in the manger, not that he was necessarily *born* there. While the animal room is called a manger, the same word literally means a feeding trough. It certainly sounds like they use that as a makeshift bassinet, whether or not she actually delivers him in the stable. To be fair, I'm not sure doing it in a crowded house would be much better. We cannot tell whether Mary and Joseph have any help or must manage independently. Luke records Mary's version of the story, so one of those two excluded such details. They focus on the remarkably humble setting where the Son of God, the long-awaited King of the Jews, arrives without fanfare.

Well, maybe not wholly without fanfare. An angel appears out of nowhere and lights up a nearby field with a pack of shepherds watching their sheep. As a quick side note, that means it does not happen in December because they would not be in the field at night in the winter. Children's pageants typically pick the pretty girl as the angel, but I think the strongest jock would be more appropriate. Angels must be intense and intimidating because they hardly ever appear without their first words being something like, "Don't be afraid." This time is no exception, and the shepherds freak out until the angel announces that the Messiah was just born in Bethlehem. A town the size of Bethlehem would not expect many babies to be born in one night, but this is the only one wrapped in cloths and lying in a manger.

Suddenly a massive crowd of angels shows up to sing the world's first Christmas carol. Or do they? We always view this as an angelic choir singing beautiful music. We already saw how intense a single angel is. Imagine when the army of Heaven shows up! The Bible calls them *"a multitude of the heavenly host praising God and saying, 'Glory to God.'"* (v13-14) For some reason, we decided that means singing, but it's more likely shouting and cheering like an army that just won a great victory.

My favorite part of the whole thing is the implied animals. One of the reasons people raised animals was for sacrifices. In those days, you could not just pray to have your sins forgiven; you had to bring a sacrifice to the altar in the temple. The guidelines are a little hazy for how often they do that, but the minimum requirement is a lamb every year at Passover. People who live far from Jerusalem usually buy one when they come to town, but those who live close enough can raise a lamb at home and bring it with them. Bethlehem is only five miles from Jerusalem, so there's a good chance this stable houses sacrificial lambs. Local shepherds most likely guard the flocks that provide sacrifices to travelers.

So, we have Jesus born in the location of sacrificial lambs, and His first visitors are the same people who watch over sacrificial lambs. That sounds fitting for a baby born to become God's sacrificial lamb for the entire world. I suspect this is the very reason Luke includes this tidbit of information. He gives so little detail about the event, which is fair because he wants to record the life and ministry of Jesus. But I wonder if he noticed that symbolism of Jesus coming into the world as a sacrificial lamb and couldn't resist giving just enough of that story for us to appreciate it too.

Singing It Wrong

Matthew 2:1-18

We three kings of orient are.
Bearing gifts, we traverse afar.
Field and fountain, moor and mountain,
following yonder star.

I love Christmas carols as much as the next guy, probably more than most people. But you need to be careful about taking them too literally. Most of them are based more on tradition and storytelling than Scripture and history. The story of the wise men is quite possibly the most misunderstood and unfairly criticized part of the entire Christmas narrative. If your understanding is based mainly on the song lyrics above, buckle up because it's almost entirely wrong.

Let's start with the easy part, the actual people. For starters, nothing ever says there are three of them.

That tradition springs from the three different gifts they deliver when they finally arrive, assuming it was probably one gift each. Eastern tradition says there were twelve of them, but Matthew never says a number. He also never calls them kings but describes them as mages, magicians, or wise men. Something more like wizards than royalty. We know for sure there is more than one of them. Considering how nervous their arrival makes everyone in Jerusalem, they may well travel with such an entourage that it looks like an invading army. Probably something along the lines of *Aladdin*'s Prince Ali Ababwa.

Finally, where are they from? Matthew says "the east," which the song calls the orient, but frankly, all it necessarily means is somewhere east of Israel. It's probably not right next door, or he would have named the specific kingdom. It's just somewhere off in the east (many scholars think modern-day Iraq or Iran), but Matthew seems unconcerned with that detail. So far, the song isn't holding up well. Then again, I freely admit *We Three Kings* sounds much catchier than *Some Unspecified Number of Magicians*.

We'll follow the Bible instead of the song, so don't worry about the gifts yet. But how about that star? Skeptics call this a fairy tale because scientists realized long ago that no star could lead them from "the east" to Jerusalem. Please get this! Matthew 2:2 says they saw the star in the east and came to Jerusalem; it never says they *followed* the star to get there. The only thing they are following is a prophecy. These guys are magicians of some sort, and astrology must be part of their practice because they observed some unidentified sign in the heavens. That could be anything in our modern scientific terms, maybe a comet or something. It doesn't need to be a literal star just because they used that word. We still refer to meteors as "shooting stars," even though most people fully realize they aren't stars at all. Something in their lore and prophecy told them that whatever they saw signaled the birth of the long-awaited Messiah, the divine king of the Jews. They set out to find and honor him, but they wouldn't need any celestial guide to lead them. The obvious place to find the king of the Jews is in Jerusalem, so they go there. We don't need to postulate some bizarre astronomical event that would last their entire journey and always point them toward Jerusalem. They saw something significant, interpreted it as a sign of the new king, and promptly went to the capital looking for him. It drives me crazy to see something so plain get so widely misinterpreted.

When they ask to see the prophesied king, everyone knows they mean the Messiah. No one is confused over which king they want, although the reigning king freaks out at word that the promised king has arrived. He asks the Bible experts where the Messiah is supposed to be born, and they tell him Bethlehem. While our wise men clearly have some knowledge of the promised Messiah, they evidently do not have the full Scripture. If they had known the prophecy about Bethlehem, they would never have come to Jerusalem instead. King Herod secretly sends them to Bethlehem with instructions to come back and tell him where the new king is, trying to use them as spies to find this threat to his kingdom. When they leave the king, suddenly they see the star again, and this time it does say they follow it. It sounds like just one night's journey, so that's not so hard to accept.

But where does it lead them? Matthew never explicitly says Bethlehem (even though some modern English translations do). He just says they follow it to "the house," where they find Jesus and his mother. They give him gifts of gold, frankincense, and myrrh. The significance and symbolism of those gifts are worth a Google, but I won't go into it now because I'm more interested in just how much they give him. These guys just traveled untold hundreds or thousands of miles, with enough of an entourage that they made Jerusalem nervous, to present their gifts. Do you think they brought little trinkets? These would be over-the-top lavish gifts, much like those the queen of Sheba brought to Solomon. That's how you honor a king. Many people have attempted to calculate the monetary value of these gifts. Few of them come up with a number less than $100 million, and some are much higher.

We don't know precisely when this happens, but scholars generally agree they don't find baby Jesus lying in a manger. Luke 2 tells us that when they dedicate Jesus, Mary brings a pair of turtledoves (or possibly pigeons). The law allowed that for a poor person who could not afford a lamb. That would have been 40 days after Jesus was born, indicating that these gifts come later. God warns the wise men not to go back to Herod, so he kills all the male children in the region of Bethlehem who are two years old or less. That age derives from when the wise men first saw the star, implying this event could be as many as two years after Jesus was born. Again, Matthew didn't consider that an essential detail, so there's not much point in squabbling over it now.

My favorite part of the story is how God spoke to these wise men. Don't miss that they were pagans practicing astrology (at least), and what Matthew calls mages may well be sorcerers. And yet, God reveals the Messiah's birth to them. They respond by worshiping the new King of the Jews through great personal effort and expense. They don't have all the answers and go to the wrong place until some scholars point them in the right direction. But after they meet Jesus, God speaks to them directly and tells them not to return to Herod. God speaks through signs in nature, through Scripture and prophecy, and even through dreams and visions. He was willing to meet them where they were and lead them to His Son. God will still meet you where you are and use whatever currently has your attention to point you toward His Son. If you will respond as they did and make a move to find him, you too can meet Jesus and be forever changed. Hopefully, if someone writes a song about it, they can get the details right!

All You Can Eat

Matthew 14:13-21, Mark 6:30-44, Luke 9:10-17, John 6:1-13

Jesus fed 5000 people from one kid's lunchbox. Sure, that's impressive, but is it all that significant? Out of all of the mind-boggling things Jesus did, how important is one meal, even if it was a miracle? Jesus said and did so many remarkable things that His life inspired more books, songs, and art than any other human in the history of the world. Yet, this unexpected buffet is the only miracle included in all four gospels. To put it another way, no one telling the story of Jesus considered it complete without this event. Why?

Let's start with some context. For Jesus and the disciples, this was supposed to be a relaxing retreat. Herod just executed John the Baptist. Jesus and John were close, so news of his beheading is a blow to Jesus. Even though Jesus knew it was coming, it is still a deeply personal loss. The locals either don't know about John or don't care. They just recognize Jesus, the guy who teaches things they've never heard, heals everyone He touches, and casts out demons wherever He goes! When Jesus and His posse get off the boat, a huge crowd awaits them. Many scholars believe it to be the largest audience Jesus ever had, right when all He wants is some peace and quiet. Rather than getting annoyed (like I would), Jesus feels compassion for them and spends the whole day teaching and healing them. When evening rolls around, the disciples recommend that Jesus should send the people away to start the long walk home, and they need to hurry if they want to get dinner in town. I have a hunch their true motive is they want some food for themselves. Jesus suggests feeding the crowd themselves and explicitly asks Philip where to buy bread for everyone. Poor Philip looks around and says it would take more than half a year's wages to give each person a single bite. John lets us know that was only a test because Jesus already has a much cooler plan.

This crowd famously numbers about 5000 men, so we usually call this story "Feeding the 5000." Don't neglect the culture behind that number. Family is a big deal to these people, and families are usually pretty big (Jesus himself has at least four brothers and two sisters we know of). Many men in this crowd probably have their families with them. Even if we assume an average of one wife and child per man (undoubtedly some had more and some less), the number is up to 15,000. We don't know exact numbers, but based on the culture and Philip's comment about the difficulty of getting a single bite for each person, it's probably more like tens of thousands. I like concerts, so I think of it this way: don't picture a crowd in front of a bandshell; picture a packed stadium. The disciples panic when Jesus tells them to feed this crowd.

While all four gospels mention the famous five loaves and two fish, the funny part is that none ever really say how they found or got them. Matthew and Luke make it sound like the disciples knew all along that they had this tiny bit of food but knew it would be preposterous to try to feed thousands of people with it. John adds a detail that Andrew brings an unnamed boy to Jesus with a snack pack. Did they know this kid before this moment? Did he hear them talking and offer it? Did they ask around to see if anyone had brought some food for the day? Did one of them spot some random kid sneaking a bite and steal his food? We have no idea. Still, I love that Andrew brings him to Jesus, well aware this is a meal for one, not even enough for the disciples, much less a multitude. (Fun fact: Andrew, Peter's brother, only shows up a few times in the gospels. But whenever he does, he is always bringing someone to Jesus. Not a bad way to be remembered!) And speaking of that multitude, just what are they doing while this whole conversation goes down? Again, we have no idea.

Jesus then tells His guys to arrange the crowd in groups of fifty. That sounds like a throwaway line, but keep in mind the size of this audience and imagine being one of the disciples trying to coordinate them. Any outstanding Bible students in attendance might start figuring it out right about now. Back in 2 Kings 4:42-44, Elisha performed a very similar miracle. That was with far more food and fewer people, but it's the same idea of feeding a large crowd with nowhere near enough food. Jesus takes the five loaves and two fish, gives thanks, blesses them, then breaks the loaves and hands them to the disciples to distribute. Nothing implies that it has multiplied at this point, so the disciples must feel ridiculous trying to offer these tiny portions to the crowd.

Somewhere in the process, the food just keeps multiplying. Once again, I dearly wish the text would come out and tell us what that looks like! This tiny amount of food is split up among (I assume) 12 disciples to distribute it, so it's probably just in their hands. Do they get to watch a piece of bread grow back every time someone breaks a chunk off? They started with only two fish. Do they suddenly have baskets full of fish? The worst thing about having this story in all four gospels is none of them explicitly tell us how the multiplication happened, and you get slightly different ideas from the separate accounts. Among many theories and speculation, the fact remains that we don't know for sure. How is it that each of the four gospel writers recognized the importance of this story, but none of them thought the mechanics of it were an important detail?

All we know for sure is everyone eats their fill. Far exceeding everyone getting a taste, the text explicitly says the people gorge themselves. You can bet that most of them are unaccustomed to such a satisfying meal. And let's face it, if you recognize each bite you eat as a literal miracle, you will probably eat as much as possible. I wouldn't be surprised if quite a few people fill their pockets too. After the impromptu feast, Jesus sends the disciples to gather the leftovers so that nothing goes to waste. They end up with twelve baskets of bread. Jesus must want to drive this point home because they each walk away with a takeout package that probably exceeds what they started with collectively. The multitude is so impressed that John tells us they want to make Jesus their king, with or without His consent. But Jesus has different plans, so He just sends everyone away and goes off to pray.

Sure, that's a nifty story, but why is it here? Jesus performed many miraculous signs, but this is the only one in all four gospels, so it must be significant. It's also one of the only miracles that Jesus personally refers back to later in His ministry. Matthew and Mark tell us about another very similar meal, this time with seven loaves of bread for 4000 men. Those numbers are slightly better than the first time, but still way too many people for their meager supplies. Once again, the disciples collect leftovers after everyone eats their fill. Later, when Jesus warns the disciples to watch out for "the yeast of the Pharisees," the disciples decide that must mean He is mad at them for not bringing enough bread with them. Jesus reminds them of both times He multiplied bread for thousands of people and asks, *"Do you still not understand?"* (Matthew 16:9 NIV)

They missed something He tried to teach them, and I believe every gospel includes this story to help us avoid making the same mistake. These miraculous meals show us how irrelevant terms like "not enough" are to God. Resources, in general, were never a concern for Jesus. He spent a lot of time teaching people what matters most, especially those disciples who were with him day in and day out for years. We tend to forget how much of that time was urging us not to waste so much mental energy on the day-to-day details of life, like what we will eat and wear. Matthew 6:33 says, *"Seek first the kingdom of God... and all these things* [that you're so worried about] *will be added to you."* God is well aware that we need those things, and, like any good parent, He is more than happy to provide them for His children.

Jesus is no fool. He knows the importance of food and shelter, but He wants us to evaluate our needs from an eternal perspective as He does. When we get all worked up over everyday details like food and clothes, we lose sight of His much bigger plans. Putting our time and energy into His mission is not just more important; it's a lot more fun. Occasionally, it gets us a front-row seat to a miracle!

Not the Best or the Brightest

Matthew 14-17; Luke 5; Acts 2-3,10

J esus called a ragtag group of nobodies to be His closest disciples who would eventually proclaim the good news of His resurrection to the world. Even in that rough crowd, Peter stands out as a loose cannon. He has absolutely no filter and repeatedly says and does the most outrageous things, seemingly without thinking. We mainly remember this wild character in snapshots of his craziest moments, like failing to walk on water or cutting off a guy's ear. Nevertheless, Jesus deliberately selects Peter as His right-hand man. He is consistently named first among the apostles and becomes their clear leader once Jesus leaves. He goes on to preach the first great message of salvation in Christ and eventually leads the world's first megachurch. Peter deserves a closer look.

We first meet him as a fisherman on the Sea of Galilee named Simon, but it's hard to tell when Simon first meets Jesus. The Bible focuses more on *what* happened than *when* it happened, so we just have to deal with the fact that sorting things in chronological order is tricky at best. We never know for sure if we get it right, so I won't even try. Sometime before the gospel narrative begins, Simon encounters this upstart preacher from nowhere named Jesus, who is making waves in town. According to John 1:42, shortly after meeting him for the first time, Jesus tells Simon he will be called Peter. And since that is the name we usually remember, we will just use that from now on.

They are barely more than acquaintances when Jesus uses Peter's boat as a makeshift stage to preach to a large crowd on the shore. (For nerds like me, the physics of sound propagation and acoustics that make that work are pretty cool, but let's not dwell on it.) After the sermon, Jesus tells Peter to head out into the lake to catch some fish. Peter had already fished all night with nothing to show for it. More importantly, he is a professional who knows more about fishing than this newbie preacher, so he knows this style of fishing works best at night. In what becomes a pattern with Peter, he voices his opinion and disagreement first but then obeys anyway. They suddenly catch so many fish that their nets start to break, so they call their partners in another boat for backup. This load of fish is so huge that it practically sinks both boats. Peter at once recognizes that Jesus is a holy man, while he himself is decidedly not. Jesus calls Peter and a few of his associates to follow Him. At the height of their career, on the most successful day they have ever imagined, they walk away from all of it to follow Jesus.

That introduction supplies a few crucial details about Peter. He speaks his mind freely (whether good or bad) and makes quick decisions. Not only is he a fisherman, but he is a serious professional and reasonably successful. He has partners working multiple boats on these waters and appears to give the orders. Far from one guy in a rowboat, he seemingly commands a fleet of fishing vessels. That position itself implies something else. Careers are practically decided at birth in this culture. Girls are barely acknowledged and certainly have no education or career options, but that is another topic for another time. Boys receive basic education in the Torah, the Books of the Law. Occasionally a rabbi (that word means "teacher") chooses some of the brightest students to follow him: to learn from him and potentially become a rabbi themselves someday. Our closest approximation would probably be getting accepted to a prestigious college. Everyone else returns home to learn his father's trade. That means these professional fishermen already flunked out of the system, effectively being told they are not good enough for God. When Jesus calls them to follow Him, He gives them a second chance. But He deliberately shows them what success in their existing career feels like and then asks them to make a choice. They know full well that this decision is permanent.

Another of Peter's most famous stories is not about fishing but still about a boat. This time Peter gets out of the boat to walk on the water. Right after Jesus feeds (more than) 5000 people with a boy's sack lunch, He sends the disciples across the lake while He goes off to pray. They end up rowing against the wind all night, most likely miserable but not scared (half of these guys are old fishing pros, remember). That changes when Jesus shows up walking across the lake. My favorite detail of this story is that Jesus initially acts like He's just walking right past them. I think He is making light of the situation to mess with them, but of course, they freak out because, well, people don't usually walk on water.

They think it must be a ghost, but Jesus essentially says, "Relax, it's me!" making Peter's response funny. "Lord, if it's you, command me to come to you." Jesus must be thinking, "Didn't I just say it was me?" What does Peter hope to prove here? I imagine a ghost could say, "Come on out," just like Jesus does. Or is Peter saying, "Jesus, that's awesome! Can I try?" Whatever the case, Peter steps out of the boat and takes at least a few steps on the water. No telling how long that lasts before the logic side of his brain takes over when he sees the waves, realizes how crazy this is, and starts to sink. I wonder if that was slowly or suddenly. Jesus, of course, saves him, and they climb into the boat. We tend to mock Peter for sinking, specifically because Jesus says his doubt spoiled it. I think he deserves more credit than that. No one else got out of the boat at all, so he is the only one who took *any* steps on the water, even if he did end up sinking.

On the night Jesus gets arrested, at their last meal together, Jesus tells them that everyone will desert Him. Of course, they all insist that will never happen, and Peter, as we would expect, goes above and beyond. He insists that he would rather die than leave Jesus, and I don't doubt that he means it at the time. Jesus calmly says that before the rooster crows (i.e., before this night is over), Peter will repeatedly deny having anything to do with Him. A little while later, Jesus takes Peter, James, and John into a garden to pray. Jesus is in such deep distress that He physically sweats blood (yes, that's a real thing, you can Google it), but the other guys keep falling asleep. They wake up when a group of armed guards arrives to arrest Jesus, and Peter starts swinging a sword. I love the irony of this moment: a groggy fisherman with a sword attempting to defend the Almighty God of the Universe. A temple servant named Malchus is probably glad Peter was half asleep. Peter cuts off the man's ear, but he was surely aiming for the whole head. Jesus tells him to put the sword away and quietly puts the poor guy's ear back on.

Without going into great detail, Peter denies Jesus three times. At the third one, Jesus makes eye contact with him from across the courtyard as a rooster crows. Peter runs off and weeps because he failed his master and best friend a few hours after being warned about this very thing. It is not much of an exaggeration to say his life is a lie at this moment, or at the very least, he feels that way. To be fair, all of the disciples feel like failures right now. We next see them three days later, all (except Judas) gathered together, hiding from the Jewish leaders. But don't miss that Peter is in that crowd. At the first report of an empty tomb, he runs to see it for himself, not even hesitating to go inside and investigate.

Peter's time with Jesus ends just like it started. Sometime after the resurrection, Peter is back to fishing on the Sea of Galilee. We can cut him some slack, though, because the angel at the empty tomb said that Jesus would meet them in Galilee, so this is honestly the right place to be. I suspect Peter gets antsy waiting for Jesus to show up, so he and his old partners head out to fish for the night, like in the old days. Once again, they catch nothing all night until a guy shows up in the morning and tells them to cast their nets again. Suddenly, the nets are too full to haul them in. Everyone recognizes this scenario and knows that guy on the shore is Jesus. After cooking them breakfast, Jesus takes Peter aside and calmly assures him that his life and ministry are far from over.

Peter started as a failure, considered not good enough to become a teacher. Then he spent three years with Jesus, messing things up more often than not and ultimately betraying his master. After all of that, he eventually leads the group of radicals who turn the entire world upside down. He is quite possibly the biggest screw-up in the New Testament and yet the focal point for the whole movement of Jesus-followers. That is the overarching message of Peter's life. No matter how often or publicly you fail, God will never cast you aside. He can still use your life to change the world if you give Him a chance.

Temporarily Dead

Matthew 27:57-28:15; Mark 15:42-16:16;
Luke 23:50-24:49; John 19:31-20:23

All of Christianity hinges on a single event, the resurrection of Jesus. Even His sacrificial death, while also massively important, is just a prerequisite for the resurrection. So many traditions, stories, and art have centered on this event in the last two thousand years that we can barely distinguish the truth from the embellishments. Worse yet, we often overlook much of what the gospels actually say, leaving us confused about the single most meaningful event in world history. I don't expect to solve that dilemma in a few paragraphs, but we will hopefully make sense of a few pieces.

Let's start with Jesus's death since we cannot call it a resurrection until we can be sure He was dead in the first place. I can't cover all the details about how, when, and why He died. All of that matters in its own right, and many of our traditions and assumptions about it are incorrect, but that's another story for another time. All four gospels, along with repeated references in the rest of the New Testament and several secular historians, assert that Jesus was crucified. Roman soldiers, who were professional experts in pain and death, publicly executed Him. If there is one thing you could count on these guys for, it was killing people. Their odds of mistaking an unconscious man for a dead man are laughable, especially considering that they received the punishment themselves if they failed in their duties. When their job was executing three men that day, you can be confident that those three men died that day. Crucifixion was nothing new to them, and they were terrifyingly good at it. Even when one of them found Jesus dead surprisingly early, a commanding officer stabbed Him through the heart with a spear, just to be sure. And a doctor (Luke) recorded the event in medical terminology, confirming precise details of exactly how Jesus died.

So, He was dead. And not just dead, but then He was buried. We typically miss how significant this is to the overall story. Burying a dead guy seems obvious to westerners like me, but crucifixion was as much about shame and disgrace as pain and death. Crucified victims were left on the cross to rot or be eaten by wild animals.

That body was officially Roman property and removing it from the cross was a crime. At this crucial moment in the story, all four gospels introduce a wealthy, influential man named Joseph from the town of Arimathea. He only gets a couple of sentences in each gospel, but Easter, as we know it, would not exist without him. They collectively portray a righteous man looking for God's kingdom. This search evidently led him to Jesus because he is also identified as a disciple (aka follower) of Jesus, although secretly for fear of the Jews. That last part is significant because he is also a respected member of the Jewish council but one of the few who had not consented to the council's decision to execute Jesus. We only know of Joseph because he finds the courage to ask Pilate (the governor who ordered Jesus's execution) for the body. Pilate is surprised that Jesus is already dead and confirms it with the commanding officer (probably that same guy who confirmed it himself with a spear). Joseph must have some influence because Pilate allows him to take the body and bury it. Again, this leaves zero doubt that Jesus is indeed dead.

Joseph and his friend Nicodemus (another respected Jewish leader who quietly followed Jesus) bury Jesus according to Jewish customs. They have to hurry because sundown is approaching, which begins a Sabbath where they can do no work. We don't know if they wash the body first, but they wrap it in linen cloth and about 75 pounds of aloe and myrrh. Even if Jesus were somehow still alive, this would suffocate him. Most importantly, they place Jesus in a tomb cut in the rock and roll a huge stone over the entrance. I'm not sure why it matters, but three gospels point out that the tomb is brand new, so Jesus was the only person ever buried there. Significantly, Joseph owns it, and people know that. Mary Magdalene and Jesus's mother watch this whole thing and know exactly where they buried Jesus. They apparently don't trust Joseph and Nicodemus to do it right because they head home and prepare their own spices to bring back to the tomb after the Sabbath. More on that in a bit.

The following 48 hours are the darkest point in history, and the Bible stays eerily silent. Man has murdered God, and the man they believed to be the Savior of the world is now a cold, lifeless corpse in a garden tomb. By the way, this is Passover, a glorious feast to celebrate God's deliverance. The disciples spend it in hiding, terrified that the Jewish leaders will come for them next. Jesus repeatedly warned them that He would be killed but come back to life in three days. If any of them remember that, they must not believe it. No one expects a resurrection. Ironically, only His enemies remember that promise, and they definitely don't expect it to happen. The chief priests and Pharisees go to Pilate and ask him to secure the tomb to prevent anyone from stealing the body to fake a resurrection.

Appearing before the Gentile (worse yet, Roman oppressor) governor is a shockingly "unclean" thing to do on Passover. That might show how important this is to them, or maybe just how much they despise Jesus that they will go to any lengths to oppose Him. It also reaffirms that the location of the tomb is common knowledge. They not only know which tomb to guard, but they assume everyone else also knows. Stealing the body to leave behind an empty tomb only matters if everyone knows where Jesus's body *should* be. Pilate allows them to guard it and seals the stone in place.

Guards and seals might be enough to prevent a hoax, but they can do nothing against the power of God. First thing Sunday morning, an angel shows up at the tomb. The text is unclear whether the guards cower in fear or simply pass out altogether. Either way, they are not *guarding* anything at this point. The angel rolls the stone out of the way and sits on it (I don't know why that detail amuses me so much). The women who watched the original burial return to anoint his body with more spices. They ponder how to get that massive stone out of the way but seem unaware of the guards. Much to their surprise, they find the stone already moved and the tomb empty.

They still don't interpret that as a resurrection until an angel shows up to tell them Jesus has risen. The angel sends them to tell the disciples, who don't believe their story anyway. Speaking of stories, those guards at the tomb report everything to the priests, who pay them off to claim they were just terrible at their job. Their official story is that the disciples snuck in and stole the body while the guards slept. That claim makes absolutely no sense because it admits a complete failure in their duties, punishable by death. Still, that's how the Jewish leaders explain the empty tomb. Note the repeated emphasis that everyone knows exactly where they buried Jesus. That conspicuously empty tomb demands an explanation.

Nothing inplies that anyone yet believes Jesus rose from the dead. Mary Magdalene is the first person to see Him as she stands outside the empty tomb, wondering what to do next. When Jesus first shows up, she doesn't recognize Him. That becomes a recurring theme when people see Him, so He must look somehow different. It also shows that He seems normal, unlike the ragged corpse Joseph and Nicodemus removed from the cross a few days ago. Don't miss the fact that a group of women first discover the empty tomb, and one of them is the first eyewitness of a risen Jesus. Most of us are too modern to realize why that matters, but this culture did not take women seriously. No one would make up a story with women as the key witnesses to your most important event. A woman could not testify in court because no one trusted what women said. Remember how the disciples didn't believe the first report from the women? Even seeing the empty tomb for themselves, they viewed all this nonsense about angels and even Jesus showing up as crazy talk from overly emotional women. When all four gospels say it was women and specifically name them, it lends serious credibility to the authenticity of this story. That detail embarrasses the very men who wrote the gospels, but they tell us the truth.

Here is where things get crazy. Jesus shows up, literally out of nowhere, inside a locked room where the disciples hide for fear of the Jewish leaders. As another embarrassing detail, Jesus has to prove He is not a ghost because they still don't believe in the resurrection. He shows the nail scars from being crucified and eats some fish before they finally believe Him. Jesus rebukes them for not believing earlier. If anyone should have trusted that Jesus physically rose from the dead, it was these guys. They heard His promise (repeatedly) that He would rise in three days. They saw the empty tomb for themselves and heard the women's story of the angels.

Somehow, we typically forget the most extraordinary evidence. Matthew 27:52-53 tells us that many old saints also came back to life. They left their tombs, went into Jerusalem, and appeared to many people. I wish we had names here, but the point is Jesus is not the only one inexplicably alive. You have people like Gideon, Elisha, and Hoseah walking around the city too. I cannot imagine why this gets so little attention. It's one brief sentence for something so shocking.

Jesus spends the next 40 days appearing to hundreds, probably thousands of people. At least once, it was in a crowd of 500 people. The sheer proximity may be the biggest reason to accept the truth of the whole story. These gospels (and most of the New Testament) were written within walking distance of the specific tomb, within the lifetime of the people who saw the risen Jesus with their own eyes. This story spread like wildfire in the exact time and place when it would have been trivial to disprove it if it was not valid.

Now that the disciples finally accept the truth of the resurrection, Jesus sends them out to tell everyone else. And He literally means *everyone*. He wants them to reach the whole world with the life-changing truth that He paid the price for all sin for all time, conquered death itself, and restored humanity's connection to God. A few days ago, the disciples swore they would follow Jesus anywhere, even to death. Then they promptly ran for their lives and huddled in a locked room, explaining away the women who showed up insisting that He was alive. But resurrection changes everything. From this moment forward, the disciples fear nothing. They face serious opposition in the form of public beatings and death threats (some of which prove to be more than empty threats), but nothing shuts them up. They simply cannot stop talking about how Jesus has changed their lives and inviting more and more people to experience it for themselves. At first, it's just Jerusalem. Then it spreads to the countryside. Soon it even includes the Gentiles (which they definitely did not expect).

The transformation and celebration endured and spread until it reached me a couple of thousand years later on the other side of the globe. I pray that it reached you too. Maybe the truth just broke through to you now in reading this story. If you want to experience the transformation and join the celebration, all you have to do is believe and say so. It doesn't matter how you say it. Just tell Jesus (He can hear you because He's alive, remember?) that you don't want to fumble your way through life anymore, doing things your own way, and you choose to follow him. You can find some advice to get you started in the final chapter of this book, but you don't have to do things my way. If you genuinely want to follow Jesus, He will show you how. And He will do a much better job of it than I can. As a far wiser man than myself put it, *"Now Jesus did many other signs in the presence of the disciples, which are not written in this book; but these are written so that you may believe that Jesus is the Christ, the Son of God, and that by believing you may have life in his name."* (John 20:30-31)

Too Long; Didn't Read

Matthew 22:35-40; Mark 12:28-34

J esus said and did some of the most amazing things in human history. If you ask random strangers what Jesus did, you'll hear of the famous miracles like healing people and walking on water. If you ask what He taught, the most common responses will probably be love and forgiveness. The abundance of lessons and events, each with its own significance, makes it hard to focus on anything, so it all blends together and gets hazy. John ends his Gospel by asserting that we could not possibly record everything He did. Well then, how much does He expect us to remember? Conveniently, people felt the same way back then, so Jesus specifically declared the most important lesson.

At this point in the story, Jesus is making big waves with His traveling teaching and healing ministry. Huge crowds follow everywhere He goes. Not everyone is a fan, though. Religious leaders and legal experts routinely oppose and challenge Him with questions. They hope to trap Him in His words to find a way to get rid of Him. One of them asks Jesus what the most important commandment is. Jesus says to love God with all your heart, soul, mind, and strength. We could dig into the precise definition of each of those terms, but I think we can agree that this means to love God with everything you have. Today we might say to love God with all of you: with every thought, word, and deed.

Jesus never seems to play by the rules in these confrontations, so He gives two answers when asked for the single most important commandment. Before they can even respond to the first piece, Jesus says to love your neighbor as yourself. This line has become a proverb in our society, lumped in with "slow and steady wins the race" or "a penny saved is a penny earned." But Jesus is not just throwing out a tweetable nugget of good advice. Matthew (written to Jews) and Mark (written to non-Jews) both record this exchange, including the second answer, so this must be just as important for everyone. Jesus doesn't even call this the second-most-important commandment but treats it like two sides of the same coin. Loving God is not the whole answer, even if you sincerely believe that you truly love Him with every fiber of your being. No matter how much you claim to love God and even show it, it will always be imperfect and hollow unless you love your neighbor as yourself.

This immediately raises two follow-up questions: who is your neighbor, and what does it mean to love them as yourself? Frankly, the rest of the New Testament is an answer to those questions. One of Jesus's most famous parables, the Good Samaritan (Luke 10:25-37), is a direct answer to the first question. Simply put, your neighbor is anyone you encounter. We are all created in the image of God, and every single human life is incredibly precious to God. The Old Testament taught both of these ideas, and Jesus repeatedly affirmed them. By that criteria, every person you meet or even hear a vague story about is your neighbor. No one is excluded from the command for you to love that person as yourself.

So then, how do you love yourself? Some people try to exempt themselves from this commandment, claiming that they need to spend time learning to love themselves first to be able to love others. That is nonsense (it should be a much stronger word, but I'm keeping it PG here). No matter how low your self-esteem falls, you still give your body food, water, and shelter. You probably go way beyond that. You cut yourself lots of slack because you know your situation.

Other people are rude, mean, or downright evil. You occasionally "make mistakes." Maybe you were a little short with that cashier yesterday. But she was venting about her troubles while you were running late for work, and of course, you couldn't take the time to be a sympathetic ear. On the other hand, when you finally got to work, and your boss just criticized you for being late and wouldn't even hear you out about how it was that cashier's fault? Well, that's because he's just a jerk.

The best description of loving your neighbor as yourself I've ever found is from C. S. Lewis in *Mere Christianity*. I highly recommend checking that out, but I'll weakly summarize it.

+ You assume you are more or less a good person, certainly not perfect but not a villain (at least you can always find an example of someone worse than yourself).
+ You trust that you have good motives and reasons for your opinions and actions. Even the worst things you've done in life all had a reason, most of it from outside circumstances and other people, and you barely see it as your fault.

- You think you deserve a little bit of grace when you make mistakes. After all, nobody's perfect.

That is how you love yourself, and it's exactly how Jesus expects you to love others. The people around you should receive the same allowances you freely and automatically make for yourself. Love like that assumes the best and forgives the worst without keeping score. It never stops at words but shows itself in acts of compassion.

Jesus made it clear that this kind of love is non-negotiable for anyone who claims to love God. The command to love God with every facet of your existence is incomplete and unfulfilled unless it includes this love for your neighbor. According to His definition, *everyone* is your neighbor. The worst person you've ever met is made in the image of God and therefore merits your love and compassion. They might not be worthy of your *trust*, and He never said to put yourself in harm's way or remain in a dangerous and toxic relationship. However, they are still infinitely valuable to God, and you should treat them as such.

This was Jesus's core message, the fundamental thing that set His teaching apart. When He knew He was just hours away from a horrific execution, He shared one last meal with His disciples and re-emphasized this lesson. He told them to love one another as He had loved them. It took a while to sink in, but they eventually got the memo. Read the rest of the New Testament and you will see countless examples of this radical new love. Indeed, that is what attracted so much attention to Christianity. Outsiders were baffled by it, many criticized and mocked it, but no one could deny it.

I fail to see how we can resist this instruction today. Jesus told us to love each other. You don't need complicated theology to understand that. John, that same guy who said we couldn't possibly write down or remember everything Jesus taught and demonstrated, boiled everything down to this principle decades later. I'll leave you with his own words from 1 John 4:11,20-21 (CEV).

> *Dear friends, since God loved us this much, we must love each other. ... But if we say we love God and don't love each other, we are liars. We cannot see God. So how can we love God if we don't love the people we can see? The commandment that God has given us is: "Love God and love each other!"*

Now What?

If you're still reading this, something must have caught your attention. Maybe the old, familiar stories look a little different. Hopefully, you're starting to see the Bible in a new light.

I don't even try to hide my desire for you to recognize Jesus as more than a charismatic person worth talking about, but the only source of true life. He plainly said in John 10:10 that He came to give us a rich and satisfying life, and the point of the entire Bible is to show that He is the only way to achieve that life. Everything else that we chase after for satisfaction and fulfillment eventually leaves us empty and frustrated. Much that starts as joy and freedom ends in regret, addiction, and baggage we carry for the rest of our lives.

Christians are usually afraid to admit it, but you do not have to completely accept everything the Bible says to experience the changed life that Jesus offers. One of my favorite preachers puts it like this, "If you simply do what Jesus says to do, your life will be better, and you will be better at life." I already admitted that I want you to become a fully committed follower of Jesus. I believe He paid the debt for sin once and for all, and He grants eternal life to all who surrender their lives to Him. I happily acknowledge Him as the only eternal Son of God who became a man to live a perfect life and die a perfect death. But all of that is *not* the starting point! Such a confession is *not* the price of admission!

According to the Gospels, His first followers did not jump straight to viewing this itinerant preacher as God. At first, they just listened to Him and wondered what it all meant. Then they returned for more because they decided His teaching was worth pursuing. Somewhere along the way, they started doing the things He said to do, which is pretty cool because instead of one rule after another, He preached love. Even then, they were following a rabbi, not worshipping Him as God. As people experienced this new concept of love firsthand, both on the giving and receiving end, they grew to trust Jesus more and more. They eventually recognized Him as more than just a teacher with good ideas, but the one genuine source of life. That mostly happened when He rose from the dead and proved that even the craziest things He said were trustworthy.

Life change begins with simply practicing the principles that Jesus taught. No sane person would honestly acknowledge Jesus as Lord and Savior without knowing Him and His character and power. Some people seem to make that personal journey overnight, while others take decades. Regardless, we all follow the same path, starting with practical obedience. That is how you get to know Him. In a culture with hundreds of laws that made it easy to tell the rule-keepers from the rule-breakers, Jesus valued the people and relationships more than the rules.

That makes religious people nervous, which is precisely why I don't want you to find religion. I want you to know Jesus. You don't need me to point out your sin. Deep down, we all know how messed up we are. We know we don't even live up to our own standards, no matter how we define them. The harder pill to swallow is how desperately God loves us. I can imagine God loving *you*, but I know myself too well to understand how He could really love *me*. And I know I'm not alone in that.

This is precisely why the Bible matters, why all of these crazy little stories matter. From a thousand different angles, they reveal how much God loves you and wants to be involved in every part of your life. You can talk to him whenever you want, no matter who or where you are. Don't know how to begin? You can simply say: "Jesus, I want to know you. Come into my life. Send your Spirit to live in my heart and heal me. Thanks for always helping me and being with me!" It truly is that simple. Then just get to know Jesus and start actually doing what he actually said.

I suggest starting with John's gospel because that book particularly shows how Jesus interacted with people and what mattered to Him. Then read the other gospels for a fuller picture of Jesus and continue to the book of Acts to see how this radical love changed people's lives and what they did next. If you genuinely want to know Jesus, He won't leave you wandering in the dark. He knows what your life needs far better than I do, so I'll leave it up to Him to tell you your next step!

About the Author

I grew up going to church every Sunday, which included this thing called Sunday School. That usually involved amazingly patient old ladies teaching Bible stories to hyperactive kids like me. Sure, that still happens today, but I did it in a day before YouTube, before PowerPoint slides, and even before VHS tapes were mainstream. They used this thing called a flannelgraph: simple pictures stuck to a board and used much like puppets. For years I chuckled at the simplicity of it all. Compared to our modern world of animation and entertainment, I marvel at how those sweet old ladies used the same few pictures to tell dozens of stories.

I claimed there was no point going anymore by the time I was ten because I already knew all the stories. Looking back, I probably did because I have always memorized things quickly, whether I intend to or not. So, by the third time I heard the story of Noah, Samson, or Baby Jesus, I could practically recite it. Many people would consider that a good thing, a solid Biblical foundation, but it eventually became a weakness. As an adult, I had difficulty reading my Bible and taking it seriously. I recognized so much of it as the same old stories from when I was a kid, so I would skim over them. I assumed I already knew this part, so there was no point in studying it very closely.

Everything changed for me the day I found myself in an impromptu debate about Jesus. I was a computer programmer, not expecting anything like this to come up out of the blue. Little did I know I worked with an orthodox Jew who emphatically did *not* recognize Jesus as the son of God. He had spent years developing his case, and another coworker suddenly challenged me to publicly defend the Christian point of view against him. Even caught off guard, I had so much Bible information ingrained in my brain that I was unconcerned. Without going into detail, let me say that getting schooled in your New Testament theology by a conservative Jew does not feel good!

That experience started me down the road of serious Bible study. I was determined never to be unprepared like that again. I had been defending the divinity of Christ and felt like I had let my team down. Although there were only a few people in the room and no one declared an official winner, I knew full well that the other guy made me look stupid. I knew his arguments were wrong, but he backed them up with specific verses, while all I had were concepts and phrases that I couldn't remember where they came from. I probably quoted the hymnal as much as the Bible, and I swore that would never happen again. I could go on for quite a while about the highs and lows of my experience:

+ Finding spectacular Bible teachers to follow (even before podcasts were a thing)...
+ Running out of motivation long before reaching the end of the Bible...
+ Becoming a counselor at the old Bible camp I attended as a teenager...
+ Reading and memorizing Scripture with friends over AOL Instant Messenger (because text messages were still expensive back then)...

About ten years into it, I gradually realized that all my learning had barely changed my life and certainly hadn't impacted anyone else. What was the point of all this? To be ready on the off chance that I got randomly challenged to another debate? So, I sought out opportunities to share what I had learned. I taught Sunday

School classes and discovered I am clearly less patient than those extraordinary old ladies from my childhood. I led Bible studies and even got to do some preaching. I loved it all. My favorite part was when people thanked me for making things clear and straightforward. Stories and passages they had known for years or even decades finally made sense, and they suddenly saw how it all applied to their lives.

When my son was born, someone gave us a "Baby's First Bible" with cute pictures and a sentence or two on each page. Of course, it was the same stories from my flannelgraph days: Adam & Eve, David & Goliath, Mary & Joseph. You know, the classics. As I read him that little Bible, I was acutely aware of how much more there is to these stories. I wanted him to know those fascinating details, but even more to see why they matter. Thus began a new obsession: mining the practical, real-world, twenty-first-century lessons from the most familiar Bible stories.

As I dug into the stories, I continually encountered the same two perspectives. One group insisted these were nothing more than cute stories with good morals, akin to Aesop's Fables. The other was convinced that only a dedicated scholar could ever understand them. Both had the same result: neither group bothered to read the Bible. That finally led me to what I now consider my true calling: removing the obstacles that keep people from reading it for themselves.

I am passionate that anyone *can* read the Bible, and everyone *should*. Regardless of your background or current circumstances, God will use stories from thousands of years ago to speak into your life here and now. You cheat yourself if you wait for someone else to read it and tell you what it means. God can use the identical text to say something totally different to you than He says to me or anyone else. That is why you have to read it yourself!

CPSIA information can be obtained
at www.ICGtesting.com
Printed in the USA
BVHW081903231222
654914BV00002B/324

9 781662 864070